PRAISE FOR
PURPOSE AWAKENING

"*Purpose Awakening* introduces a fresh and revolutionary way to find your purpose in life. Touré gives a simplistic road map and personally guides you to discover what makes *you* significant. Anyone seeking purpose needs this book in his or her life."

—Israel Houghton, Grammy Award–winning singer, songwriter, and producer

"For many of us we are lost until we discover our God-given purpose. Pastor Touré gives us the blueprint to reach and maximize our true potential and walk in our purpose with excellence! Great read!"

—Niecy Nash, comedian, actress, TV personality, and author

"*Purpose Awakening* is a must read! It reinforces what many of us already feel: that there is an ultimate purpose for each of our lives. And Pastor Touré really drives this idea that we are all on a divine path home! This book will not only enlighten you, it will also inspire you to walk confidently in discovering your true purpose."

—Kelly Rowland, Grammy Award–winning singer/songwriter and actress

"*Purpose Awakening* helped me to confront things that I could no longer ignore! My life is forever changed!"

—Michelle Williams, former member of Destiny's Child

"Pastor Touré Roberts is one of the premiere leaders of this generation. *Purpose Awakening* is a life-affirming revelation of the divine power of God. It's a must read for anyone desperate to know the 'why' behind their creation!"

—DeVon Franklin, author of *Produced by Faith*

"There's nothing more important in a person's life than to find out why they're here. Touré Roberts brilliantly coaches his readers into their own purpose awakening and the awe-inspiring joy and fulfillment that follows. This is one you won't want to put down."

—Traci Lynn Blackwell, a leading network television executive

PURPOSE AWAKENING

PURPOSE AWAKENING

Discover the Epic Idea That Motivated Your Birth

TOURÉ ROBERTS

New York Boston Nashville

FaithWords
Hachette Book Group
237 Park Avenue
New York, NY 10017

www.faithwords.com

Printed in the United States of America

RRD-C

First Edition: March 2014

10 9 8 7 6 5 4 3 2 1

Contributing Editor: Crystal Flores

FaithWords is a division of Hachette Book Group, Inc.
The FaithWords name and logo are trademarks of Hachette Book Group, Inc.

The Hachette Speakers Bureau provides a wide range of authors for speaking events. To find out more, go to www.hachettespeakersbureau.com or call (866) 376-6591.

The publisher is not responsible for websites (or their content) that are not owned by the publisher.

Library of Congress Cataloging-in-Publication Data

Roberts, Touré.
  Purpose awakening : discover the epic idea that motivated your birth / Touré Roberts. — First Edition.
    pages cm
  ISBN 978-1-4555-4837-8 (trade pbk.) — ISBN 978-1-4555-4838-5 (ebook) 1. Christian life. 2. Life—Religious aspects—Christianity. 3. Meaning (Philosophy)—Religious aspects—Christianity. I. Title.
  BV4509.5.R625 2014
  248.4—dc23
                                        2013027727

Purpose Awakening *is dedicated to my three miracles who motivate every good thing I do. Ren, Teya, and Isaiah— I love you and here's to you!*

CONTENTS

Part I

THE *YOU* BEFORE YOU

Chapter 1

YOU WERE AN EPIC IDEA BEFORE YOU WERE BORN

Chances are if you picked up this book based on the title and are reading these words, you're likely someone who has already begun to question what the purpose of your life is. You've probably read books, been to seminars, and even had someone stand in front of you—all smiles—making purpose-finding seem so easy. But even after you've tried those things, you're more than likely still in the same place at the end of the day, saying, "When is it really going to happen for me?" You're serious about doing whatever it takes to find your purpose, but up to this point you haven't discovered the meaning of your life.

If this is you, I'd like for you to consider something. What if the reason you haven't found your purpose has to do with the way you've gone about looking for it? Maybe you've been taught, like so many others, that in order to discover your purpose in life, you have to take into account: (1) what you currently like, (2) what you are currently motivated by, or (3) what you presently feel. Perhaps you've been led to believe that somehow there were clues to discovering your purpose in each of these.

What if I told you that your purpose may not have anything to do with those things or what you are currently inclined to do? What if I told you that finding your purpose is really about discovering the thought that was in God's mind before you were born? A thought so amazing, it was His sole inspiration for bringing you forth. When you discover this thought, you will have found your purpose.

The Before

"Before I formed you in your mother's womb, I knew you." (see Jeremiah 1:5)

When it comes to discovering your purpose, it's important that you understand from the onset that the *plan* of you predated the *birth* of you. You began as a brilliant thought in the mind of God. This thought was so profound that it alone motivated Him to bring you into this world. When He thought about you, who you would become, and what you would do, He smiled within Himself and said, "Now that's good!"

Everything in life has a *before*. It all has to start somewhere. This is even evident in all areas of science. If you think about it, to progress forward in science is really to look back with more precision. Science teaches us that in order to understand what presently is, we must attempt to look back and discover what was. As knowledge in science increases, we come to understand what took place in the before and why.

Just as the world has a before, so do you. We often get so preoccupied with the *here and now* that we fail to consider that our life has a before. It's in this realm of the before that we find the plan for our life—the blueprint, and the schematic containing everything that is, was, and will ever be. As we lay hold of these plans, it enables us to skillfully navigate the here and now.

Before the Before

At the beginning of everything that is, was, and will ever be is God, the embodiment of flawless brilliance. The Creator, being motivated by a passion to extend His essence to an unformed world, does so with meticulous detail. He created the world we now see, and the pinnacle of that creation is you! God is the ultimate craftsman. He has shaped each of us with a precision that transcends anything that can be found. Nothing about you was created in vain or lacks significance. You have been designed with perfect intentionality.

David says it best in one of his Psalms:

You formed the whole of me, inward and out. I am awesomely and wonderfully created. Your creations are spectacular. You skillfully designed me. You saw the essence of me before I was formed. Before I existed, all of my days were written in Your book. (see Psalm 139:13–16 NIV)

Not only did God fashion you, but He knows you more intimately than anyone else.

Although the two of you may have yet to be introduced, you are no stranger to God. The One who formed you is perfectly acquainted with all that you are, all that you were, and all that you will ever be.

God is intimately acquainted with the *idea of you* that predated you. After all, it was His idea to begin with. God has seen your beginning, He has seen your middle, and He has seen your end. He knows your life inside and out.

It's kind of like people who become huge fans of a celebrity. This type of fan knows all about the person they admire. They know where she shops, what she wears, what she drives—even down to what she likes for breakfast. They are into all the details of that celebrity's life. They follow her childhood, they know about past relationships, schools she attended, and the list goes on. Sometimes these fans know more about the celebrity than even her closest confidantes. This level of knowledge and familiarity creates an intimacy, even though in this case the celebrity doesn't know the fans. Believe it or not, it's the same thing between God and us. Even when we don't know God, He knows us. He is our biggest fan. He knows every strand of hair on our head, He knows our entire story, and He longs for the day that we awaken to His friendship.

Not only does God know you, but as the earlier passage points out—He has *ordained* you. To be ordained means to be divinely designed for *something*. When God ordains something, He is exercising His divine prerogative to bring about what He desires. Everything God ordains, Heaven backs up. That thing you've been ordained for is guaranteed to work—if you do it. It is your unique shape that is distinct from any other shape on the planet. There's a space in the universe that fits you perfectly. It's your divine DNA strand. It is your eternal fingerprint. "This is going to work!" God exclaims as He puts the final touch on your design. As a matter of fact, it's the only thing that will work, anyplace, anytime, for all your days. This is the *It Factor* concerning you. This is the thing that sets you apart from everyone else. This is your calling card. This is your uniqueness. This is Heaven's interpretation of you. And in your unique identity, there is provision and divine resources. All of creation is waiting for you to find your purpose and live it out. Discovering what you have been ordained for opens up the resources of the universe to you. If God ordained it, there is nothing that can stop it. It has to happen. It must work. It will work. And that is why you must find it.

Chapter 2

LOST IN TRANSLATION

Purpose is a very powerful, yet mysterious, concept. It's the underlying question we all have deep down inside. There are no easy answers to the question of purpose, and it will never be a "quick fix" in life. It's so much more than that. Discovering your purpose is everything.

It's not my intention to sell you a pipe dream or prescribe a five-step guide to discovering your purpose. I am not interested in taking you on a ride that leads you nowhere. We get enough of that in life already. Pay close attention to these next three words: purpose isn't easy. Purpose will challenge you. It often requires letting go of former ways of thinking. There may be ways you've felt about yourself that you're going to have to change. There may be things you've come to learn about life that you are going to have to unlearn. There may even be ideas you've had about God that are going to get challenged. The truth is, discovering your purpose may cost you everything. But it'll be worth it. Whatever you have to go through, whatever you have to give up, and whatever ideas you have to cast aside won't compare to the life you'll experience when you find out what you're here for.

Now, this chapter gets a little deep, so you're going to have to stay with me. If you stick with it through the end, insights about your purpose will open up like never before. All right—let's go for it!

The easiest way for me to illustrate the concept of purpose is to bring you into a dream.

Imagine you go to sleep at night just like any other night. But tonight your dream-life takes you on an unexpected journey that will change your life forever. In your sleep you're taken on a high-speed ascent, higher and higher until it seems like it will never end. Just when you think you can't go any higher, you burst through a clear film and immediately come to an abrupt stop. On the other side of this film, you find yourself in an atmosphere of overwhelming peace, calm bliss, and an awakening like you've never experienced before. You have literally broken through, from one plane to the next, and have transcended into an entirely new realm. In an instant your mind is opened. Your state of awareness becomes a profound *knowing*. With this knowing you find yourself reconnected to something that you had lost. But before this encounter you didn't even know that what you found had been missing. After this moment of absolute peace, joy, and clarity, you feel yourself being grounded back to earth again, and suddenly you wake up. Now, in your real life, you wake up enlightened, empowered, and radically changed forever. Where there were countless questions before, now there are none. You feel whole and complete. You have a clear understanding of why you're here and what you're supposed to do in life.

This is a dream I actually had that awakened me to my purpose and changed my life forever. But I've found that my dream wasn't just about me. It was also about helping others come into their own awakening.

Let's look at the dream again. Remember that part when you broke through the film and immediately were reconnected to something you had lost, but didn't know it was lost until you found it? Well, what had been lost but later found was purpose. When you broke through the film after your high-speed ascent, the new realm you entered into was *the before*. This is where the original thought about your life was conceived.

Before you were born, you were in perfect union with God's idea of you. This means that the discovery of purpose is actually a reuniting between *you* and your *purpose*. That's why, as the dream illustrates, once you and your purpose were reconnected, everything made sense, and all of the mystery surrounding your existence disappeared. The truth is, all the answers to every question about your life are contained in the knowledge of your purpose, which is found in *the before*.

When I experienced this breakthrough for myself, a newfound confidence emerged. I came to realize that everything around me has meaning, and now nothing is irrelevant. I'm inspired in every moment of every day because I know there's a connection between my present circumstance and my purpose in life.

Understanding the Two Realms

Finding purpose is about getting back to that place where you and purpose were one. When God says, "Before I formed you in your mother's womb I knew you," He speaks of two different realms; the *before* realm and the *present* realm. The *before* realm is the eternal, invisible, timeless realm. This is the realm where creation exists, but only in thought-form. The *present* realm is the visible realm of creation in physical-form after the thought has been manifest. Creation in physical-form is the world we live in. Here we can actually see and touch the things that are around us. It's important to understand that our *visible* world first began in the *invisible* realm.

Scripture illustrates this point when it says,

> *By faith we understand that the worlds were created by the word of God, so that the things we now see were made by things we cannot see. (see Hebrews 11:3)*

The things we see in our world today were created by things we don't see. This passage confirms that there are two realms that each play an essential part in the process of creation. The *invisible* realm, where creation begins, and the *visible* realm, where creation materializes.

Purpose gets misplaced in the process of our translation from existing solely in thought-form to being manifest into physical-form.

Let's understand this process of translation. First, we know that everything begins as a thought in God's mind in the invisible realm. This thought determines the *what* and the *why* of what is being created. When you are a thought in God's mind before you are born, He knows the cause of your life and who you will be. His idea concerning you *is* your purpose. **It's the epic idea that motivated your birth.**

This means that all of our lives began as a purpose. When God looks at you He sees His purpose for creating you. He doesn't just see you as your name or your job or how others may look at you. From God's perspective, there's more to each of us than our credits, résumé, or our birth name. He sees His epic idea, which is the sum total of who we'll become in life, and refers to us accordingly. Our truest identity is our purpose.

The Geography of Purpose

Although our purpose began in the heavens, it was always intended to be carried out on the earth. In order for this to take place, we, at some point, had to take on a physical form. The translation that causes our birth is a process in which a physical form is "put around" our invisible purpose, allowing us to enter into this physical world and accomplish what we were designed to do. *This is the process where our purpose gets misplaced.*

Here's why...

Before we were born, we were solely connected to purpose in thought-form. In the *before* realm there was no physical world to compete with our awareness of our purpose. Our purpose got lost in translation because once we were born we began to connect more to the physical world by our physical senses. The five senses (sight, hearing, touch, taste, and smell) limit us because they only connect us to the things that exist in the physical realm, not in the invisible realm where purpose is clear.

The physical world is a catch-22. On one hand it's the stage where our purpose must be played out. On the other hand it's an environment that often distracts us from the very reason we were brought here in the first place.

Remember, the knowledge of purpose is found in the *before*. This is where faith comes in. Faith allows us to see beyond the physical world and into the invisible one. It's like a sixth sense that transcends the natural realm and allows us to see into the spiritual realm where purpose began.

Rediscovering Purpose

Somehow, we've come to believe that purpose is something we must discover for the very first time. The truth is, we don't really discover purpose, we are awakened to it. It's always been there.

It's not really purpose that gets *lost* in translation, but our *awareness* of it.

The fact is, purpose has never gone anywhere. It's been with us since the inception of the idea of us. *We* may have been lost to *it*, but *it* has never been lost to *us*. In fact, the One who gave us our purpose has hidden the knowledge of it deep down in the heart of each of us.

Solomon illustrates this point masterfully.

I have seen the God-given task with which we are to be occupied. God has made everything beautiful in its time. Also He has put eternity in our hearts. (see Ecclesiastes 3:10–11)

There are three main ideas about purpose within this passage. The first idea is that God has placed our purpose in our hearts. In this verse God is describing our purpose as eternity. He's referring to the *entirety* of our lives and how our past, present, and future all come together to fulfill the epic idea for which we were born. He places purpose within our hearts to be His access point to us, similar to a homing device just waiting to be awakened. God did not invest His epic idea in us unwisely. His commitment to instill purpose into the very fabric of our hearts is His guarantee, that no matter how lost we may get, we'll always have a way back to His epic idea for us.

The second idea seen in the passage is that God challenges each of us with the task of discovering what that purpose is. There will always be nagging questions inside of us: *What is my purpose in life? Why am I here? Am I living out the life I'm supposed to live? Am I doing the thing I was born to do? Is this my destiny?* And even those people who don't realize they are asking purpose-related questions will ask, *Am I doing what's right or am I missing something?* Until you know what your purpose is, these questions will be endless. It's every person's duty to find out why they are alive.

Lastly, the most encouraging part of this verse is when God says, "He *made* everything beautiful in its time." This means that the fulfillment of "making everything beautiful" takes time. It's not something that happens overnight. As a matter of fact the epic idea itself spans your entire lifetime. When God says, "Before I formed you in your mother's womb I knew you," He's speaking of knowing the entirety of you and all your days. This is how He sees you. Not only by who you are at five years old, thirty-five years old, or seventy years old, but His definition of you is the *entirety* of you. Knowing that everything is beautiful in its time is an encouragement to all of us. Even if we haven't discovered our purpose yet or don't know how one scene in our life connects to another, in the grand scheme of things everything will be made beautiful. The epic idea concerning you is a masterpiece. Once all has been discovered, realized, and carried out, the end result is everything God intended for you.

The Spiritual Birth

There is one last point here that I think is very important. This point was made in the dream at the beginning of this chapter. Remember the part when we ascended upward and finally broke through the film that brought us into this new atmosphere of overwhelming peace? Breaking through that film resembled the process of the water breaking in a natural birth. This is a significant parallel to understanding the process of discovering purpose.

Think about the process of your creation. It begins with the thought in God's mind concerning you, then leads to God placing you in your mother's womb, and finally results in you being born into this physical world. This is the natural birth. It begins in the *spiritual* and is born into the *natural*. However, there is a second type of birth that must occur in order to awaken you to purpose. This birth *begins* in the natural, but then *awakens* you to the spiritual. It's like a birth in reverse. This is illustrated in the dream when we broke through the film on our upward ascent into a new realm of awareness. This is the *spiritual birth*. It is critical because it brings you back into the awareness of the *before* realm, where you and purpose were perfectly one. Even Jesus spoke of this as the Scripture records Him telling us to be "born of the spirit" (see John 3:5–8).

Everyone discovering purpose will experience not only a natural birth but also this spiritual birth. I'll explain this spiritual birth in more detail later; however, it ultimately happens as a result of a person's authentic hunger for God and His plans for their life. If you haven't experienced it yet, at the perfect time, God will draw you to receive this amazing gift.

This is the beginning of your purpose awakening. It positions you to perceive specific instructions about your purpose and allows you to participate in walking out God's epic plan for your life.

Chapter 3

THE BOOK OF YOU

No one goes to a movie just to see the end. In fact, you don't even think about the ending of a movie until it draws near. What makes a movie exciting is what you experience while you're watching it. You get into the characters, you enjoy the story-line, the challenges and obstacles keep you interested, and most of us appreciate a triumphant conclusion.

Similarly, you don't read a book just for the end. You read a book for the journey. What makes a book great is when its story stimulates you and keeps your interest. The story of your life is no different. Just like there is an awesome idea concerning your life, there is an equally awesome story to go along with it.

There are Scriptures that tell us that all of our days have already been written. One passage brilliantly illustrates this idea by capturing its essence within the lyrics of this song of David.

> *Your eyes saw my substance before it was formed. And in your book all the days fashioned for me were written, when as yet there were none of them. (see Psalm 139:16)*

In the before realm there is a *book* that contains every detail of your life. This book is God's master plan for fulfilling His epic idea for you. He didn't leave you here without instructions to guide you, but it's your job to find your book, read it, and apply it to your life. This will keep you from a lifestyle of randomness, and instead, you'll experience a fulfilled life with the satisfaction of being in purpose.

One awesome thing about your book is that it's a success story. It contains the winning formulas for your life. God is the author, and He has made *you* the hero of the story. Your book is fail-proof and was written for you to prosper. God said Himself,

> *"For I know the plans I have for you," declares the LORD, "plans to prosper you and not to harm you, plans to give you hope and a future." (Jeremiah 29:11 NIV)*

Your story is already written, your stage has been set, and the intentions for you are good. The only thing left for you to do is find your book, read it, and apply it.

Finding Your Book

Every book ever written came from the mind of its author. The thoughts of the author were then written out to create the book. The *Book of You* is the story that God specifically wrote for your life. The only difference is, God doesn't write your book on paper; it's written in His thoughts. Therefore, in order to discover your story, you must tap into the mind of God.

Now you might be thinking, "Wait a minute, isn't this close to blasphemy? Can a human being really know the brilliant mind of the all-knowing God?" That's exactly what I'm saying. According to Scripture, the answer is yes.

> *God reveals to us through His Spirit. Now, we have received the Spirit who is from God, that we might know the things that have been freely given to us by God. (see 1 Corinthians 2:10, 12)*

This verse lets us know that the primary role of the Spirit is to reveal the things that God has written for our lives. When we enter into relationship with God, the first thing we receive is His Spirit. It is His Spirit that remains with us forever, leading and guiding us into all truth in every circumstance and season.

The Spirit of God is what gives us the unique ability to hear God's voice. For some, the whole idea of hearing God's voice is a mysterious thing. Many people live their entire lives thinking God never talks to them. This is far from the truth. The fact is God speaks to us all the time. We just have to learn how to recognize His voice.

What I've discovered is that hearing God's voice is a natural part of us. We experience it throughout our entire life. It's just that we often call it something else. Sometimes we call it intuition, sometimes we call it our conscience, and other times we just call it a "knowing." It's so much a part of the fabric of our existence that it just *is*. When we connect that "knowing" to the fact that it's God's voice, we can then apply His instructions with confidence. As we do this consistently we build a healthy relationship with the voice of God.

Although there are many people who are experiencing a healthy relationship with the voice of God, I've also found that there are others who are more inclined to fall into one of these three categories: (1) those who hear from God but don't *know* they hear from Him, (2) those who hear from God but *question* whether or not they heard from Him, and (3) those who hear from God but *don't want to* hear from Him. Those who don't want to hear from Him usually are those that lack an understanding of the character and person of God.

The most misunderstood and largely misrepresented person in the whole universe is God Himself. I have a standing joke among my friends and congregation that God has the worst PR ever.

God is often perceived as one who wants to take away your freedom, keep you from having fun, and make you the most boring person on the planet. There is nothing farther from the truth. I learned this for myself when I surrendered to God's voice for my own life. I now live the most exhilarating, adventurous, and liberated life that a person could live. I've never been happier, I've never known more joy, and I feel no sense of loss whatsoever—only tremendous gain.

Yet when most people think of the word *surrender* they envision something completely different. They see themselves giving up freedom and personal liberties. Take for example what happens when people surrender to the authorities. They are taken into custody, locked up, and have their freedoms restricted. This is the exact opposite of what happens when we surrender to God's voice for our lives. When we do so, we surrender *into* liberty, freedom, and a life of open doors and endless possibilities.

God doesn't have a hidden agenda. He makes it very clear that His ultimate desire is to see all of His children succeed. There's no other reason for God to be in our lives. His commitment to us is indescribable. He blesses us, He protects us, and He guides us. He wants to see us whole in every way. Our challenge, however, is to trust Him enough to allow Him to be the captain of our ship.

God doesn't want to restrict us. His purpose is to free us. He wants to show us infinite possibilities. When we follow God's voice, it unlocks our potential, unfolds our destiny, and allows us to realize His epic plan for our life.

Finding the *Book of You* is about finding the voice of God.

God Speaks to Everyone

There are people today that believe God has never spoken to them and feel they have never heard His voice. There's nothing that God wants more for us than to know that He speaks to us. On the other hand, there's nothing that *doubt* wants more than to convince us that God doesn't.

Think about this. God gave us eyes that allow us to see His

majesty in creation, ears to hear sounds and melodies that stir our hearts and souls, and mouths to taste fine foods of the earth that delight the heart. This all communicates that God is consumed with us. When we consider the great lengths He goes through to reveal His splendor to us, it becomes unfathomable to think that He would decide not to speak to us.

Just look around and you'll see His majesty in a sunset, a sunrise, all the beauty on dry land, and all the treasures of the sea. These creations reveal God's fingerprints on everything around us. He is so infatuated with us and so longs for us to know Him that He puts a reflection of Himself in every part of creation. When you consider all of this, it is impossible to believe that He would have us live our entire lives without saying anything to us.

Just because we *feel* that God has never spoken to us doesn't mean He hasn't. It's just a matter of recognizing His voice and learning the ways He communicates with us.

Your "Inner-Knower"

Everyone has what I like to call an "inner-knower." This is your *organ of perception*. Just as we have organs that cause our physical body to function properly in the physical world, God has given us a spiritual organ that allows our spiritual body to function properly and perceive spiritual truths. Your organ of perception is what connects you to God's voice.

All of us have it, but we must recognize it, develop it, and utilize it or it will lay dormant. Too many people live their entire lives full of unrealized potential because their organ of perception is ignored.

This spiritual organ is your built-in discerner of God's voice. Check out this eye-opening passage on the subject:

Those who are mature, and who by reason of use, have their senses exercised to discern both good and evil. (see Hebrews 5:14)

The first thing I'll point out here is the root meaning of the word translated as *senses* in the passage. It comes from the ancient Greek word *aistheterion* (a-hee-shtay-tay'-ree-on). The literal translation of this word is "organ of perception." This word has only been used one time in the entire Bible. I believe this speaks to the unique and rare nature of our organ of perception.

As we look further in the passage we see a connection being made between our organ of perception and spiritual maturity. This is because discerning God's voice requires a commitment to spiritual growth. Confidently perceiving God's voice clearly doesn't happen overnight or by mistake. It requires effort and intentionality. It's a process that doesn't come cheap, and it shouldn't—it's an endowment to be cherished. We're talking about divine intelligence here. With just one word, God can release revelation and knowledge that give us keys to unlock amazing things in our lives.

Sometimes what is holding a person back is their inability to unlock the mystery in a situation that is hindering them. Often the greatest source of frustration in life isn't a particular problem, it's our inability to understand it and solve it. It's in these moments when God's voice becomes the problem-solver. There are times where we may feel stuck and unable to progress, but when His word is spoken to us, it becomes the key that unlocks that scenario and allows us to move on to the next level in life. That's why knowing that we have access to God's voice gives us confidence and assurance. It means that no matter what circumstance we find ourselves in, all we have to do is find His voice and He will give us the best advice on what to do next.

Discerning God's Voice

The first step to discerning God's voice is the commitment to the idea that *you can*. As I mentioned earlier, there is nothing that God wants you to believe more than that He speaks to you. At the same time there's nothing *doubt* wants more than to get you to believe that He doesn't. You *can* hear from God, but you have to overcome the thought in your mind that tells you that you can't.

There's a passage that says, "As a man thinks in his heart, so is he" (see Prov. 23:7). In order to be a discerner of the voice of God, you are going to have to become a thought-regulator. God's voice will always have to compete with other thoughts and ideas that will attempt to bombard your mind. To be a successful discerner of God's voice you will have to develop a lifestyle of fighting against every other competing thought. Now right here is where you might ask the question, "Well, if I have all these competing thoughts, how do I know which one is God's voice? How do I know it's not my own thought? How do I know it's not doubt speaking? How can I decipher between the voices?"

The answer is simple. You have the organ of perception. God has placed within you the ability to *perceive* His distinct voice. He's made this promise very clear in Scripture.

> *My sheep hear my voice, and I know them, and they follow me.* (John 10:27)

You will always have a way to connect to the voice of God. You just have to be diligent in silencing the other thoughts.

Fine-Tuning Your Hearing

Growing in your ability to discern God's voice happens through the process of trial and error. There will be times when God speaks to you, yet you are uncertain about whether or not you heard properly. Depending on how you respond to what you hear will determine the outcome. If you hear properly and follow accordingly, you will experience a favorable outcome. At other times you may be unclear or fail to heed the message. In this instance the outcome can be less than what you would desire. These outcomes become God's training ground that teaches you how to best discern and follow His voice. Ultimately, sharpening your ability to perceive God's voice happens after countless times of hearing it, responding to it, observing the outcomes, and adjusting accordingly.

I recall a time when I first started my church and God spoke an unusual instruction to me. At the time, the church was only two years old and had grown to become a whopping thirty-member megachurch! We were located in the greater Los Angeles area when God spoke to me and told me to uproot from that region. The only problem was all of my members lived and worked there. The new area was in a completely different part of town, where most of my members almost never visited. If there was ever a time for selective hearing, this was it. I sat on this information for a while until I recognized that God's instruction wasn't going anywhere. I wasn't getting past "Go" unless I did what He said. In every place I turned and in every conversation I had, I could hear the voice of God reminding me of what He was asking me to do. Finally after a couple of months, I preached a sermon about how all of us need to step out in faith. After the sermon was over, I conveniently introduced my intentions to move the congregation out of the area. You could hear a pin drop. I'm a pretty fiery speaker, and I'm used to getting a lot of "amens" and "hallelujahs." On that day, all I heard was crickets. Nevertheless a huge burden had been lifted off of my shoulders. I knew no matter how difficult the decision was, it was the right thing to do because God told me to do it. I stepped out in faith, and the fruit of that decision was an enormous growth in our membership and the ability to reach far beyond what I could have ever expected.

All this happened as a result of making one decision to follow one instruction I was able to hear because I tapped into God's voice. In addition to learning how important it is to hear God's voice and follow it, I also realized that God's plans for us are so beyond what we can see for ourselves. If we are willing to relinquish our own dream, trusting that God's dream is bigger, He will show us things that are far beyond what we can ask for or even imagine.

Lastly, I want to point out that there are numerous ways your organ of perception can tap into God's voice. God has placed His voice in many things that are all around you. God has a million ways to speak to you. I have even experienced God's voice coming to me through the saying of a three-year-old child. When we are able to recognize God's voice in whatever channel He chooses, and are committed to following that instruction, we will then experience a fruitful existence of success and fulfillment as we seek out His epic plan for our life.

Part II

BEING SET APART FOR GREATNESS

The Three Levels of Separation

Chapter 4

LEAVING YOUR FATHER'S HOUSE

Now that you understand there is an epic idea that motivated your birth, it's time to dive in deeper. This is where your passion for purpose must take over in order to realize the great destiny God has planned for you. The first practical step to realizing your purpose begins with embracing one word— separation.

> *Now the LORD had said to Abram, "Get out of your country, from your family and from your father's house, to a land that I will show you. I will make you a great nation; I will bless you and make your name great; and you shall be a blessing. (Genesis 12:1–3)*

You can't have greatness without separation. In fact, greatness itself means to be separated from the norm. It means to stand out from the crowd. Greatness makes a decisive statement separating the ordinary from the extraordinary. Your purpose in life is what makes you great, but in order to accomplish that greatness you must be willing to accept separation.

The hardest part of pursuing your purpose is separating yourself from *the familiar* and stepping into uncharted territory.

The story of Abram above illustrates that the first practical step in pursuing purpose is leaving behind the familiar.

The Trap of the Familiar

The greatest threat to your future is the familiar. Too often people sacrifice their dreams because they are afraid to leave behind what they've always known. The familiar is the often subconscious thought that the predictable is the preferred path, and that the recognizable is the best option.

The familiar takes pride in being settled in what has always been. It is adverse to anything new, even if that means settling into mediocrity.

From our youth, we're raised on sayings like, "if it ain't broke why fix it" or the classic "a bird in the hand is better than two in the bush." These clichés have reinforced the trap of the familiar by suggesting that what has always been is greater than the possibility of what could ever be.

The above Scripture is the introduction to an amazing story about the life of a man named Abram. This story tells of him venturing forth and following God's instruction to leave his familiar surroundings and to pursue the epic plan God had for him. Abram's decision to listen to God's voice changed his life dramatically. In the passage God gives Abram clear instructions on how to carry it out. Let's take a closer look at Abram's interaction with God to glean some pointers that anyone seeking purpose can apply.

Stepping Out

When God engages Abram with the instructions for his journey, the first thing He tells him is to *GET OUT*.

At first glance, these words may not appear to be motivational or inspirational, but in reality they are. When God purposes to move you to the next level, it always requires an exodus from a former place of comfort.

God adamantly tells Abram from the onset to *GET OUT*. Why? Because He knew Abram could never *step into* his destiny without first *stepping out* of his complacency. What God envisioned for Abram's life was so enormous that it couldn't fit into his current situation. When God wants to bring you into your purpose, the first thing He will tell you is to "get out." This is God's way of saying, "This promise I'm making about your future is so big that it won't fit into the place where you presently stand. I need you to move out from where you are and into my vast open plane where I will reveal to you my epic plan for your life. My vision for you is too big for your current surroundings."

In spite of the hope and future that *getting out* promises, actually doing it is another story. The fear of the unknown, or sometimes just complacency, can paralyze us. This can cause us to remain in a place or a season too long, at a time when we are required to step out. Fortunately, God's plans for our lives aren't subject to our readiness to take the plunge. I can recall a time in my own life when God, shall I say, "helped me" into my future.

Early in my professional career I was abruptly let go from my position with a company that I had planned to grow old in. It was my dream job with a large national corporation that promised great opportunity for advancement with several career path options. The pay at the time met my needs, I had good benefits, and for all intents and purposes, I was satisfied. What I couldn't see, however, was the lurking storm heading toward the shores of my stability in the form of a termination I didn't deserve. Without provocation I was fired, and I was devastated.

My world was rocked not only because of the shattering of *my* plans, but what made matters worse was that I didn't understand why.

What I couldn't see at the time, however, was God at work behind the scenes. What I had believed to be a major setback, I soon discovered was really just a set up for a major step up. After accepting what I couldn't change and moving on, in just a few months, I found myself in a new career, earning more money, with a shorter commute, and on my way toward the greater plans that God had for me. None of these blessings could have come had I not been forced out of my complacency. Oh, and the best part of the story was this: after nearly a year's time, the former company uncovered their mistake that led to my termination. They apologized profusely and offered me my job back with retroactive pay. One of the most satisfying moments in my life was pulling up in my brand-new car, receiving the check that I was due, and then telling them they couldn't afford me anymore. I'll never forget that day.

The beginning of promotion and elevation will sometimes look like failure and misfortune, but God is always up to something good in our lives.

What's Shaping You

In God's instruction to Abram, He reveals the second key maneuver to walking out purpose—leaving behind the familiar.

> Get out of your **country** from your **family**, and from your **father's house** to a land that I will show you.

Here, God identifies three factors that have a substantial impact on all of our lives. These factors determine how we see ourselves, how we see others, how we believe others see us, and how we relate to life as a result.

At this very moment, our identities are the by-products of how these things, called *the familiar*, have shaped us. The things that are most familiar to us are: (1) our **country**, also seen as our environment, culture, and subculture; our customs; and our styles of communication, (2) our **family**, which encompasses relatives, the broader community, and familiar acquaintances, and (3) our *father's house*, which involves assumed or predetermined expectations.

Each of these things are part of our familiar, which is the predominate shaper of our identity. But at some point you have to leave *this* place of shaping in order to be shaped by God according to *His* purpose for your life.

Leaving the Familiar Behind

Although it's possible for positive shaping to happen in the familiar, it will always have limitations. When your familiar is the only thing shaping you, your growth is automatically capped. This is because in the familiar all of your life's exposure is limited to a certain amount of common experiences. The familiar is what you've grown accustomed to. When you have any culture, a community, or a subculture, what makes it a "culture" is the repetition of the same experiences. There's no growth—only recycling, which produces a shortage of new ideas and creates predictable expectations.

Leaving the familiar is leaving the place that is presently shaping you and stepping into a new realm with a plethora of new experiences God uses to *reshape* you for your destiny. Remember, in order to realize purpose you must become a "you" that you haven't met yet, and you can only do that when you leave the familiar.

This was the case with Abram. When God engaged Abram with the great plan for his life, He knew the only way to get him to even fathom new possibilities was to expose him to brand-new experiences.

In essence, God says, "The place you're in now will not shape you for all that I have in store for you. A significant part of being shaped for destiny will come by what you experience through your relationship with Me. Your life began as an epic idea in *My* mind. I brought forth that idea, and called it *you*. You are My child, and I want to teach you a new way of thinking and show you a new way of living. I want you to reconsider some things about your life. You may understand the facts of your life, but I can reveal to you the *truths*; truths that existed before you were born. You may have knowledge about your life, but I have the hidden wisdom that motivated your life. Come with Me as I lead you out of the land of what's always been and into the land of the never been seen before. It's here where all things are possible."

Stepping into the Land of God

*Now the Lord had said to Abram, "Get out of your country, from your family and from your father's house, **to a land that I will show you.***"

The most fascinating thing to me about this story is that Abram actually leaves. Can you imagine being told by a voice to leave your place of familiarity and comfort, and journey into the unknown with nothing more than a promise? That's a hard pill to swallow, yet Abram, who was later called "The Father of Faith," did exactly that, and reaped unfathomable rewards for doing so. The same will be true for you as you leave behind the familiar and allow God to lead you to the land that He will show you. When God is giving Abram this promise about a land, He is not just talking about a physical land, although that was included. He is also speaking about a unique spiritual environment of shaping that becomes the setting in which your life is formed for purpose and destiny.

There are five key things that happen in God's land that shape you for purpose. Let's take a look at them.

1. You Increase

Several years ago, I learned a fascinating lesson about the *power of environment* through a pet turtle. For years this turtle remained the same size and never grew. One day I noticed the turtle was much bigger than I had remembered. When I asked my friend who owned the turtle about the sudden growth, she said, "You'll never believe this. I used to keep the turtle in a small tank. Then I got him a larger tank, and all of a sudden he grew!" What blew me away was that the growth of the turtle was dependent upon the size of his environment. We can all stand to learn a valuable lesson from this turtle.

You can't grow any bigger than the environment that is presently shaping you. Your growth limitations are determined by the surroundings you subject yourself to. There is no greater environment for growth than the infinite planes of God. Stepping into God's land takes the limits off of what is possible for your life. It is the perfect staging ground for the discovery of the epic idea that motivated your birth. It isn't until you step into God's land that you realize how limiting your previous environment was.

This epic idea can only come forth in a setting large enough to cultivate it. The size of your environment also determines the bounds of your creativity. Your creativity is a key part of you fulfilling your purpose. Your creativity is your potential. When your potential is fully maximized it's called purpose, which is the epic idea that motivated your birth. In order to fulfill your purpose in life, you have to dwell in environments that unlock your potential and releases the creativity that God has placed inside of you.

2. You Discover Your Real Name

From the time you are born you're called something. This ranges from terms of affection as a child to your given name as you grow older. Sometimes people used nicknames, and sometimes they even "called" you names. When you get married you may change your name, and some performers even have stage names. No matter what, you're always being called *something*. But have you ever stopped to wonder what God calls you? Have you ever paused to consider that maybe you only have one name? And no one truly knows that name except the One who created you. What if there is a name that is the embodiment of all that God had in mind before He put you in your mother's womb? Guess what? There is.

When God approaches Abram, He calls him his *true* name, by telling him what his destiny would be. Let me explain. If you read further in the story, you'll learn that God changed Abram's name to Abraham. This happened after Abram left his father's house and stepped into God's shaping process. When God tells Abram to leave the familiar, He also tells him what's going to happen in his life and who he will become once he does.

Here is what God says to him:

"I will make you a great nation; I will bless you and make your name great; and you shall be a blessing. I will bless those who bless you, and I will curse him who curses you; And in you all the families of the earth shall be blessed." (Genesis 12:2–3)

When God makes the proclamation "in you all the families of the earth shall be blessed," He is giving Abram his *true* identity. God was telling him that He was making Abram a father that would be a blessing to all the people throughout the nations of the earth. In God's mind your true identity is always linked to what He knows about your future. Once Abram embraced the identity that God placed on him, God changed his name from Abram to Abraham, which just so happens to mean—you guessed it—"father of many nations." And this is exactly what Abraham became.

God's vision for your life will always be so much greater than what you think. When He gives you your identity by revealing to you your destiny, don't resist it. Although it may be bigger than where you currently are, embrace it. You'll find that when you do so, just like Abraham, you will become it.

Abraham had to leave his father's house in order to discover the true identity that awaited him in God's land. If there's no other reason to get out of your father's house, it's to find your identity and the purpose that's assigned to it.

3. You Learn to Trust God

Walking out your purpose in life will require an unwavering trust in God. The challenge is, trusting God can be one of the most difficult things to do. What's great is that this difficulty is no secret to God, and He often does things to earn our trust. You may not know this about God, but He doesn't always expect His children to trust Him blindly. He longs to do life with us, and through experiencing God's consistencies, our trust in Him gets established.

God called Abraham to enter into the unknown because that's where he'd learn to trust God completely. What began as an instruction from God to leave the familiar became a lifelong journey of experiencing God's faithfulness. This journey was a successive cycle of God speaking, Abraham believing, God delivering, and Abraham's trust increasing. One of the primary reasons God calls us into His land is because it contains countless scenarios that give us the opportunity to build our trust in Him. After witnessing a consistent pattern of God coming through for you, trusting Him becomes your way of life.

4. You Learn Yourself

The hardest thing for us to do is to see ourselves truthfully. Each of us has an idea of the type of person we are, but there is a difference between who we think we are and what our life is truly speaking to those around us. That's why it's important to always have truth-tellers around you. Truth-tellers are people who love you enough to tell you the truth about yourself. They have nothing to gain from you and only desire to see you do well in life. They have no risk in telling you the truth, and because you both know this, you trust what they say and take it to heart. But the greatest truth-teller about who we really are is the environment God places us in when we leave our father's house.

You'd be surprised by how many things are uncovered about you when you leave the accommodations of the familiar and are exposed to new and sometimes uncomfortable environments. Things you never knew were in you come to the surface, or if you did know these things existed, you'd always found a way to justify them. The truth is, we all have an unlimited capacity for self-justification. This makes it critical to sometimes be placed in lone environments with God, where we have to ponder tough questions about ourselves to gain a truer perspective about who we really are.

I've had several experiences of this very thing. This calls to mind a time when I, as a young husband, was having a difficult time in my marriage. The challenges at that time became so intense that we separated and lived in different homes. One night I came home to my empty, lifeless apartment, which once was the same place I enjoyed the company of my wife and the laughter of our children. Although it was the same home, everything felt different. I remember walking into a dark room and accidentally stepping on my daughter's squeaking rubber ducky. It was once a part of my nightly bathing ritual with my daughter—our own special moment we shared together. Greatly missing those moments, I was overwhelmed with emotion and began to sob.

Alone in that place of brokenness I began to ask God to show me the truth about myself, and He did. For the very first time in my life I began to see not the ideal me, but the real me. Not the person I thought I was or longed to be, but the person those near to me were experiencing. I'd never been more devastated, yet also inspired at the same time. Although God showed me some very ugly things about myself, there was hope because I now had the opportunity to be the man I truly wanted to be. Sometimes, to become who you want to be God has to show you who you often are.

Please understand something. God never shows you who you really are to harm you, but to help you. Had he never shown me who I was being to my wife and family, I could never have made the adjustment to become a better husband and father. God didn't condemn me or make me feel ashamed—He just told me the truth. He just loved me forward as He often does. Love without truth is not love. Truth without love isn't the whole truth. Love and truth are inseparable. God's love in telling me the truth about myself made me the man I could never have been if He hadn't. This experience also taught me the valuable lesson of balancing confidence with constant self-examination.

Abraham experienced many lessons in God's land. He learned about his fears, overcame them, and later became a very courageous patriarch. He discovered that he had many doubts, but he went on to become the Father of Faith. Discovering the *real you* is a vital step to overcoming obstacles that hold back your purpose. Learning yourself is a major reality in God's land.

5. You Grow Up

There isn't a greater teacher in life than experience. The things that we experience in God's land are priceless and make us great. In God's land we increase, we learn our real name, we learn how to trust in God, and we learn ourselves. Because all of these things happen to us in God's land—we grow up.

Your destiny requires your maturity. It requires you to *become*. Your *becoming* happens as you walk with God in His land. Your highest self is formed there. The more God shows you, the more you change. You get better at listening to Him, and great things start to happen for you. Life starts to become an awe-filled and exciting adventure. Once you leave the familiar and continuously experience the goodness of life in God's land, you will never want to go back.

I'm certain that if Abraham was asked on his deathbed what was the best decision he'd ever made in life, he would confidently and reminiscently say, "Getting out of my father's house."

Chapter 5

HONING THE GIFT OF "GOOD-BYE"

Your father's house and the familiar aren't the only things that you'll have to say good-bye to on your journey to purpose. There will also be times when you have to part ways with individuals, groups, and even family members to be positioned for the epic things God has ordained for your life. The second level of separation involves the necessary discipline of leaving relationships, when the situation or season requires it. Saying good-bye to people can be the most heart-wrenching task, yet it must be done at times to preserve the plans God has for you.

I want to say early on that saying good-bye to a relationship is not about the other person—it will always be about you. Separating yourself is never to vilify another person but instead to establish you in your own purpose-walk. The truth is, relationships matter. How you align yourself with people, or not, will determine the doors that will open up for you and the doors that will remain closed. Making adjustments in relationships can be very difficult, but we have to do it. If we do, we'll avoid many headaches, we'll keep from losing valuable time, and believe it or not, in some cases, doing so will even save you money.

Even our buddy Abraham had to exercise the *gift of good-bye*. His journey involved a pivotal moment of separation that became the catalyst for the fulfillment of his destiny. Let's take a look at the story:

> *Then Abram went up from Egypt, he and his wife and all that he had, and Lot with him, to the South. Abram was very rich in livestock, in silver, and in gold. Lot also, who went with Abram, had flocks and herds and tents. Now the land was not able to support them, that they might dwell together, for their possessions were so great that they could not dwell together. And there was strife between the herdsmen of Abram's livestock and the herdsmen of Lot's livestock. (Genesis 13:1–2, 5–7)*
>
> *So Abram said to Lot, "Please let there be no strife between you and me, and between my herdsmen and your herdsmen; for we are brethren. Is not the whole land before you? Please separate from me. If you take the left, then I will go to the right; or, if you go to the right, then I will go to the left." (Genesis 13:8)*
>
> *And the LORD said to Abram, after Lot had separated from him: "Lift your eyes now and look from the place where you are—northward, southward, eastward, and westward; for all the land which you see I give to you and your descendants forever. And I will make your descendants as the dust of the earth; so that if a man could number the dust of the earth, then your descendants also could be numbered. Arise, walk in the land through its length and its width, for I give it to you." (Genesis 13:14–17)*

Abraham's separation from his close relative Lot is a great example of how parting ways, when necessary, will mean everything to your destiny. Let's glean insight from the story to help us understand when separation is required and how to walk it out in a productive way, with the least amount of collateral damage.

The Symptom of Conflict

Although not every conflict ends in separation, most separations begin with conflict. Sometimes conflict is used to teach us valuable lessons or to mature us, as in the case with young marriages. When a marriage first begins, it's important that the couple doesn't *give up* before they *grow up*. In other cases, however, conflict communicates to us there's disagreement somewhere in a situation or relationship. This lack of agreement is the initial sign that a separation is ahead. In the story, conflict arose between Abraham's group and those who were with Lot. A telling phrase in the story lets us in on the real problem. The phrase states that "the land was not able to support them that they dwelt together."

I don't believe that the land being referred to here is about square acreage or square mileage. The earth wasn't any smaller in Abraham's time than it is today. As a matter of fact there would have been even more space for them to dwell together then, because of a smaller population at the time. The deeper meaning of "land" has to do with the environment that God called Abraham to step into in order to fulfill his purpose. In other words, there wasn't enough space in Abraham's destiny for Lot to walk with him. Sometimes two people cannot fit into one destiny. The journey was about Abraham's purpose, much like you reading this book is about yours. God knows who is written in the *Book of You* and who isn't. He knows who is written throughout your entire book and who is relegated to just one chapter. When an individual's chapter in the *Book of You* is ending, God will allow conflict to awaken your awareness to it.

Conflict for purpose's sake is not only the beginning of separation—it's the proof that separation has begun. The farther you walk into your destiny, the more there will be an organic pushing away of the things that no longer fit. At the same time there will also be an organic pulling together of things that do. Sometimes the conflict is clearly evident and at other times the conflict is just an inner knowing. Whether the conflict is undeniably apparent or just an uneasiness within, the next step must always be confrontation.

It Won't Just Go Away

There was a time in my life that I noticed a common tendency among several members of my family. They all held back their thoughts and emotions. You couldn't get anything out of them unless you pried open the door to their feelings with a crowbar of questioning. It was like you needed a secret passcode to get to what was really on their mind. The interesting thing about it, however, is that most of these family members believed they were doing everyone a favor by keeping things to themselves and "avoiding conflict." What they didn't realize was that they weren't avoiding conflict at all, because the conflict was already present. They just suppressed it. As a result, the conflict remained within them, causing them to be deprived of peace and freedom. It also left them with the emotional instability of a complicated inner struggle. This is not the way to live. Conflict must always be confronted.

It wouldn't surprise me one bit if Abraham delayed the uncomfortable separation talk with Lot for a period of time. Can you imagine having to say good-bye to someone you've known your entire life? Lot was even there when Abraham made the challenging decision to leave behind the familiar, and he was also by Abraham's side when he journeyed into the land of the unknown. This would have certainly complicated Abraham's angst about parting ways with Lot. Sometimes the guilt you feel about letting go of someone who was there for you in a difficult time will blind you to the fact that now the relationship itself has become the difficult time. It's moments like this when you have to realize that separation is not about the person you're saying good-bye to. It's about saying hello to, and embracing, the awesome plan that God has for you.

Remember, the first part of the word *good-bye* is good. It's good-bye, not bad-bye. There is as much *good* in ending the *wrong* relationship as there is in beginning a *right* one. There are ways, however, to make certain that your process of separation is a good one and has the least amount of collateral damage. The first step in the good-bye process is to acknowledge the conflict.

Abraham knew that this conflict wasn't just going to disappear. He knew it had to be addressed and also sensed what the only resolution was. Abraham faced the situation with Lot head-on, and by doing so was able to move forward into his purpose. He wasn't in denial about where things were and neither can we be when we find ourselves in similar situations.

I can recall a time in the past when I began to feel separated from a couple that was part of my staff. There was nothing visibly obvious that brought about a sense of conflict, but I couldn't shake the alarming inner-knowing that something wasn't quite right. The couple had been close companions for several years, making it easy for me to shrug off the notion that any serious conflict existed. So I did what most people do—I suppressed the conflict I was feeling inside, and I would later pay for it.

What eventually was uncovered was that this couple had developed bitter emotions over time, and they began to sow seeds of bitterness into others in our organization. I found out later that these things were happening at the same time that my good-bye detector had been sounding off. While I was in a state of denial, the issue only got worse. The elephant in the room grew larger and larger until ultimately what I had been feeling in my heart was being exposed plainly in my sight.

My response, of course, was to give the couple their long overdue good-bye. When I did, not only did the strife and conflict cease immediately, but our organization experienced a great season of growth and success. However, because of my initial season of denial, I was left to clean up a mess that would have been avoided had I moved sooner on what I already knew. That experience taught me many things and helped me to hone and sharpen my own gift of good-bye.

It's Called Good-Bye, Not Get Lost

In your pursuit of purpose there's no way around having to separate from others, but how you say good-bye is very important. One thing to always remember is that on the other side of your good-bye is another human being with feelings. People should never be regarded simply as stepping-stones to get you ahead, nor dismissed as nothing more than obstructions to your destiny. Neither one of these notions can ever represent the true, full identity of any other person. Everyone has their own story, and their life is shaped by many factors that make them who they are. The same God that made you also made them, and He has a great plan for their lives too. Recognizing this will determine *how* you say good-bye when that time comes. The best way to say good-bye is in a way that not only promotes your forward progress, but also releases the other party into all God has for them. Remembering this will ensure that your road to destiny isn't paved with a trail of maimed bodies in your rearview mirror.

Abraham demonstrates this beautifully in his interaction with Lot at their moment of separation. In the story, he employs four essential aspects necessary for anyone seeking to have a healthy and successful good-bye. Here is what they are.

1. Honesty

Telling the truth isn't always easy, but it will always be right. Abraham doesn't misstate or water down what the issue is. He is direct and truthful about the conflict between his herdsmen and Lot's herdsmen. He doesn't make it about something it's not. He gets straight to the point. At the end of the day people want us to be honest with them. Many times there's an opportunity for them to grow because of the feedback we give them. You can never let your fear of hurting someone's feelings keep you from telling them the truth.

Even if a person's feelings get hurt temporarily, in time they may very well return and thank you.

2. Honor and Affirmation

Next on the list of must-haves in your good-bye is honor. There isn't a better time to affirm someone's worth to you than at the time of separation. In the story, Abraham affirms Lot by saying to him "for we are brethren." In essence Abraham is saying, "I care about you. You are valuable to me. Let's not allow anything, even our relationship, to stand in the way of our mutual honor and respect for one another." This is huge in the good-bye process. Humans need affirmation at all times. There are so many opportunities in life for people to feel rejected or not good enough and their most vulnerable time is in a moment of good-bye. It's important to say kind things to people and to encourage them about their future when letting them go. Find two or three things about them you think are amazing and celebrate them. Bring up those things when you are saying good-bye, and tell them how awesome they are. Granted, you may have to invest more time searching for these qualities when dealing with some people, but as a rule of thumb, keep in mind that people are more than their personalities. Although we can't completely control a person's feelings when we are saying good-bye, we should do everything in our power to make people feel valuable.

3. Generosity

It's also key to be generous when saying good-bye. When leaving a relationship, the person on the other end will undoubtedly feel a sense of loss. They will feel like something is being "taken" from them, possibly causing panic and the fear of a void. Not only will affirmation help them cope with this sense of loss, but being generous will also go a long way. In the story, Abraham graciously offers Lot first choice of all of the land that was in front of them. He says, "Is not the whole land before you? If you go to the left, I'll take the right. If you go to the right, I'll take the left."

Not only did Abraham affirm Lot in the bright future that was in front of him, he also tells him to take first pick in choosing whatever he wanted. Whenever possible you should always have a parting gift when saying good-bye. This could be a thank-you card thanking them for their friendship over the years. It could be a plaque honoring someone in your organization whose season to move on has come. In some cases you could choose to relinquish your rights or shares in a business endeavor that has ended. It could be choosing to forgive a person's debt on your way out the door. There are a number of things that you can do to demonstrate your generosity, all of which will go a long way in cultivating a healthy good-bye.

Here's something to remember: **you will only be generous when you are convinced about the prosperity of your own future.** If you don't believe that things are going to work in your favor, you will try to hold on to as much as you can. Never fall into this trap. When you separate, remember you are saying good-bye to what was so you are available for the promotion ahead. There's an upgrade in your future waiting for you. It's similar to a yard sale. In a yard sale, someone is clearing out the old to make room for the new. You hardly see anyone haggling over prices at a yard sale. The seller is more interested in parting with the old thing than in turning a profit. The season for those items has expired. In some cases sellers will actually *pay you* to take the item away, because in their mind they've already envisioned something greater.

Abraham could be generous, and not feel loss by doing so, because he knew that God had greater things in store for him. When you are convinced that your future has already been funded, you'll have no problem investing in your good-bye. Being generous at the point of your separation is a down payment on the new life and the destiny that God has for you.

4. Decisiveness

The most essential component to a healthy good-bye is actually going through with it. You have to be able to close the deal. The good-bye that leads to destiny too often is sabotaged because of indecisiveness. Maybe you've been here before. You were sure this was the right thing when you prayed and consulted the wise, but when you actually tried to say good-bye, things got blurry. Or maybe you went through with the good-bye, it lasted for a season, but you began to question your decision because of loneliness and uncertainty. The optimism of your newfound freedom got eclipsed by the fear of the unknown, and finally the comfort of the familiar pulled you right back into the very relationship that wisdom told you to leave. These are all-too-common scenarios in the good-bye process and must be avoided in order for you to be separated for greatness.

Abraham was decisive in his good-bye. Notice that, although he gave Lot a choice in which direction he could take in the separation, the separation itself was not on the table for discussion. He was clear in his decision, and—most important—he executed.

Too often people get talked out of their good-bye by the one they are saying good-bye to. Somehow the person saying good-bye is coerced into thinking that if the other party doesn't agree or understand, then the separation is inconclusive. There is nothing further from the truth. Your good-bye should never be based on someone else's agreement with it. You are not responsible for whether or not the other party understands or approves. The other person "getting it" isn't your job. Sometimes the person will take it very hard and attempt to put their pain on you. Never allow this to happen. You should always be compassionate, but be careful to not allow someone else's crisis to become your emergency. Your role is to communicate your good-bye as clearly and as graciously as possible, and then to walk away.

I've seen people that leave unhealthy relationships carrying a great deal of unnecessary guilt because the other person didn't want it to end. Some people were even accused by their disgruntled exes of harming them and ruining their lives when they said good-bye. These things just aren't true. Honing the gift of good-bye is about seeing through falsehoods like these and shaking off any false guilt you may be feeling. You being separated for your purpose will never harm other people. It will help them, if they respond properly. You have to take charge of your own life, your own future, and what you believe God wants for you. Your destiny is not a joint venture. By all means be honest, be honoring and affirming, and be generous. But most of all—be decisive.

There will be times when you don't fully understand why you have to say good-bye, but don't let that stop you. You have to trust that God is seeing farther down the road than you are. Everything isn't always immediately apparent but the future will reveal all. Sometimes God will speak through an inner discomfort, telling you to separate from someone because He sees who that person will become at a higher altitude on your journey. God sees everyone's heart and intentions at the deepest level—even their future intentions. God sees things we would never see, so we have to trust our good-bye detector at all times. In the case of Abraham and Lot, the future did reveal that Lot had flaws in his character that would have slowed Abraham down. Thank God that he had the faith and the fortitude to say good-bye, and to stick with it.

Reinventing Relationships

Sometimes a good-bye won't mean a complete severing of a relationship. It will just mean that a relationship needs to be reinvented or repositioned. Relationships are reinvented when change comes to someone's life in a relationship that mandates a shift in how the person relates to others moving forward. When a relationship is being reinvented, the parties must begin to consider who they are and where they are headed. Everything about the relationship goes into a sort of auditing and evaluation stage. With newfound clarity, they are able to see what fits into their new reality and what does not. Sometimes this means that the interaction in the relationship must change to be consistent with the new direction. This will affect the *type* of interaction in the relationship as well as the frequency with which they interact.

A repositioning in a relationship is when things evolve that require a change in where people fit into your life. This has to do with relationships and roles. In the previous season, a person may have been your closest confidant, but in the new season, someone else is better suited for that role. Your circle of relationships can be compared to a basketball team. All good coaches know that there will be times when they'll have to switch up the dynamic of the players to ensure the success of the team. Every game isn't won by the starting lineup they've always had. There are times when the coach pulls an unknown from the bench to secure the victory. It's the same in relationships. Sometimes we have to say good-bye to the positioning of relationships in our lives. Good-bye, no matter how it is to be played out, is a necessary factor in moving forward.

Abraham exercised his gift of good-bye, and his reward for doing so was unfathomable. Let's recall the outcome:

> *And the LORD said to Abram, after Lot had separated from him: "Lift your eyes now and look from the place where you are—northward, southward, eastward, and westward; for all the land which you see I give to you and your descendants forever. And I will make your descendants as the dust of the earth; so that if a man could number the dust of the earth, then your descendants also could be numbered. Arise, walk in the land through its length and its width, for I give it to you."*

What an amazing outcome! God gives Abraham an incredible vision of destiny the moment he follows through with separating himself from Lot. It's as if God was waiting for Abraham to make this necessary move, and then opens up the fullness of his destiny to him as a reward.

God tells Abraham to lift up his eyes *now* and look. God says "now" because He knew Abraham would see differently now that Lot was gone. As a matter of fact, the name Lot is derived from the Hebrew word *lowt*, which literally means "veil." When the wrong people have a significant place in your life, you can be *veiled* from seeing the good that's right in front of you. Sometimes the negative or limited perspectives of others will cause *your* view of destiny to be obstructed. This is why separation becomes a vital component to your purpose. Remember this—in order to achieve it, you must first see it. When Abraham says good-bye to Lot, the heavens open to him and God reveals to him an incredible vision of his future.

This awesome story ends with God telling Abraham to arise and walk forward into the great destiny He promised to give him. Abraham was now able to look forward and become inspired by the vast possibilities that awaited him. God wants to do the same for you. Saying good-bye to something that doesn't have purpose-potential is often the greatest challenge that a person will ever face. The flipside, however, is that the right good-bye will catapult you forward into purpose unlike any other decision you will ever make.

The gift of good-bye is honed gradually from one separation to the next. Trust me—you'll have plenty of practice to learn this skill, because the higher you evolve in your purpose the smaller your circle becomes. As you grow in purpose, your life becomes less random and fewer relationships are relevant to the reason for your existence. Keep in mind, however, that how you say good-bye is just as important as the good-bye itself. Your life should always be an inspiration to others, even when letting someone go. Be honest, affirming, and generous, but decisive, and before you know it, the hard part will be behind you. You will look up and find yourself beyond the uncomfortable transitional period of separation, and will be filled with clarity and hope as you walk into the fulfillment of God's epic idea for your life.

Chapter 6

BREAKING OUT OF THE PACK

Discovering purpose and living out the epic idea that motivated your birth in some ways is like running a marathon. If you've ever watched a marathon, the race begins with a crowd of runners tightly jammed together, and moving restrictedly because there's no clear path for each runner yet. Then when the crowd breaks, you start noticing the distinctions of each runner as they settle into their unique running form, stride, and pace. Now, instead of a crowded pack of runners bumping into each other searching for an open lane, you start seeing clusters of smaller groups forming, united by equal athleticism and similar running style. As the race continues, the individuality of each runner is further defined as the group shrinks smaller and smaller. Finally, one runner successfully breaks out of the leading pack, proving his or her ultimate distinction from every other runner, and wins the race. The key to winning the race of purpose, and fulfilling the epic destiny assigned to your life, is learning how to constantly break out of the packs and the molds that life tries to keep you in.

We all begin our lives in packs of commonality and similarity, but with time and experience we begin to discover the things that set us apart. As the years pass by, we discover ourselves, and begin to better understand the life that we're meant to live. This causes the lane of our purpose to open to us, and we start running our race with focus and intentionality, breaking out further and further away from the pack until we cross the finish line of our destiny.

Although fulfilling purpose requires that you break out of the pack, it's important to know that the pack itself is a necessary part of the process. There are things that happen to your life in the pack that are key to the fulfilling of your destiny. I'll explain what I mean, but first let's give definition to the term *pack*.

A pack is a group, environment, season, or situation you are placed in temporarily, to develop and prepare you for progress on your road to purpose. In other words, it's a stepping-stone and like such, you step on it, gain balance, establish your footing, focus forward, stretch yourself, and leap ahead to the next plateau. It's a necessary place, but not a place you remain in forever. You have to move on from it in order to get where you're going. Packs have two primary functions: to train you and to establish your distinction.

The Pack Is a Great Teacher

The first function of the pack is to teach, train, and establish you for purpose. It's similar to the schooling process. The educational system has an end goal in mind—to educate you to ultimately become a successful member of society. It's designed to teach and train you gradually toward that end. It doesn't teach you everything at once, but it seeks to develop you in a balanced way by training you step by step. Grade school is significant, but you're not intended to stay there forever. While there, you learn critical fundamentals that become the foundation that prepares you for higher levels of learning and becoming. Grade school gives you the foundation for middle school. Middle school builds from there and creates the educational foundation you need for high school. High school does the same for college—college for grad school, and on and on. This much-needed process of incremental learning, growing, and establishing could not work without a key component—graduation. Between each level, there has to be a separation from the previous one—a breaking out of sorts that acknowledges that the former was just a stepping-stone to set up what's next. When it comes to purpose, breaking out of the pack is when your heart tells you deep down that you've received what you were put in that environment to receive, and now your purpose mandates that you move on.

Breaking out of the pack isn't always easy. As we've discussed before, anything that involves leaving or saying good-bye will most likely be challenging, no matter how *gifted* you become at doing it. The more difficult scenarios of separation are the ones that require you to break out of packs that involve people. When the time comes for you to do so, that infamous "false guilt" can arise in your heart about those being left behind. Somehow in your mind you interpret your upgrade as their downgrade. This guilt can be so convincing that it tempts you to shrink who you are and become less, in order to fit into a space you know you've outgrown. There is little that saddens me more than seeing a destined soul make decisions that cause deformity to their purpose; all because they were riddled with guilt about graduating in life and feared what others might say or think.

If you don't retain anything else from this chapter, I need you to embrace these two very important no-nos. Never accept a feeling of guilt for God's promotion in your life; and never allow the fear of being misunderstood or criticized to hold you back from greatness. There are few great men and women I know of who didn't have to learn this lesson. I know this lesson firsthand and had to learn it early, on my path to purpose.

There was a season in my life when I was rapidly developing in my spirituality and relationship with God. At that time I was a young minister at a church my family was very instrumental in establishing. For a season, the church gave me the challenge I needed to maintain the momentum of my spiritual acceleration. However, as time passed, I noticed the environment I'd grown accustomed to was no longer supporting the rapid pace of my spiritual growth. This created a huge inner conflict for me. I became overwhelmed with guilt for my feelings of discontentment. After all, who was I to think I had outgrown the very environment that facilitated my introduction to God? How could this community of great men and women I've always admired, no longer fulfill my thirst for spirituality and purpose? I found myself plagued with these thoughts and could hardly sleep, wrestling with these questions. Then, when I thought things couldn't get any more confusing, trusted influences from the church volunteered their "two cents" about my dilemma. When they finished talking to me I was left second-guessing myself and wondering if what I was feeling was just youthful pride getting the best of me. This was one of the most difficult times of my life.

But in the midst of my inner turmoil, perplexing thoughts, and the external voices in my ear, I could still hear a resounding affirmation deep within confirming that breaking out of this pack was the right thing to do. Every time I allowed my mind to agree with what my heart was already convinced of, I felt tremendous freedom, joy, and optimism about the future that awaited me.

Today, when I reflect back on that pivotal time, a sobering reality grips me. Had I not overcome the guilt and fear that I faced in that moment, I'd still be stuck in that pack with a far less impactful story, if any at all. Soon after breaking out of that pack, the exciting future I'd envisioned became my reality.

The Pack Reveals Your Distinction

The second and perhaps the most purpose-related function of the pack is to reveal your distinction. When you're put into a pack, it isn't for you to conform, but to learn what makes you different. The pack is designed to cause your uniqueness—the thing that makes you *one of a kind*—to rise to the surface and stand out from the crowd. You aren't supposed to lose yourself in the crowd. You actually find yourself there.

Have you ever had an acquaintance you believed strongly resembled a certain celebrity? I mean you would swear up and down this individual looked just like that certain person. But when you put the two of them together you realize they look a lot less alike than you originally thought. The closer their proximity, the more their distinctions became evident. It works the same way in the pack. The pack is the place where you begin to notice what makes you special and unique. Every human being is a distinct masterpiece. Nothing about you is unoriginal. You weren't formed on an assembly line that uses common parts, but were hand woven and brilliantly crafted out of the essence of God Himself. Every detail about you has meaning and significance and must be embraced by you, before anyone else will.

Remember, there's no one on this planet like you for a reason. No one before you was like you, nor will anyone be who comes after you. You are it. There was only one *you* mold made; after you were formed its mission was complete and it vanished. Your life is the result of a brilliant idea in God's mind. His brilliance is infinite, and He never recycles great ideas. There's only one you and that you is beyond amazing. No one can be a better you than you, and the best you emerges when you embrace your distinction.

Embracing Your Distinction

Make certain to never see your distinction from others as a drawback but as an advantage to be embraced and celebrated. The pack that you are presently in, needs you to be you. When you discover what's different about you it adds value to your pack, as well as to society at large.

There's little that hinders finding purpose more than trying to fit in when you're designed to stand out. Fitting in will never lead you to your purpose. To the contrary, when you discover your purpose it causes the universe to fit itself around you. You've probably heard the saying that the world doesn't revolve around you. Well, in a way the world does and here's why. There is a single unique space in the universe that no shape other than yours can fit into. When you find your purpose and walk in it, you fit perfectly into that space and the whole world will take form around you.

One of my favorite passages of Scripture states that "creation eagerly waits for the manifestation of the children of God" (see Rom. 8:19 GW). What a brilliant passage! It lets you know that the entire universe is anxiously and excitedly waiting for you to discover your distinction. This is a deep and mysterious truth, yet the fact remains that your distinction must be revealed, and the pack is designed to bring it to the forefront.

Being Confident in Your Distinction

Okay, let's be real. Being different can be a little scary at times. Having confidence in your own uniqueness can be a great challenge. It takes a lot of guts to say, "Hey! I'm different from everyone else on the planet, and that alone is what makes me amazing." But the fact is, that's exactly right! It's your distinction—your unique difference—that makes you incredible! This is one of the things I love about working with artists in Hollywood. They get it! There is something on the inside of the creative person that knows their distinction is their greatest asset. It's the same in the world of branding and marketing. The successful brand distinguishes itself from all other similar brands. Their strategy in doing so is to create a memorable imprint of the product in the consumer's mind. This product distinction gets highlighted and ultimately convinces us to buy. Your distinction is the brand that heaven has ordained for you, and when you start embracing it, others will follow suit. You must always be the number one fan of you.

This doesn't mean that you won't have to combat thoughts that arise to discourage your distinction. Sometimes thoughts will come that cause you to question the value of your difference. *What if my distinction isn't good enough? Her distinction is better than mine. What if I get rejected?* Thoughts of not being special enough and the fear of rejection will always work against you discovering and embracing your distinction. These thoughts seem to pop up out of nowhere because of insecurities that haven't been dealt with. Other times these "anti-you" thoughts are the by-products of hurtful things people have said to you, causing you to question yourself and the worth of your distinction. As a matter of fact, sometimes the very thing that people made fun of or discouraged you about will be the very thing that ends up making you great.

When I was growing up, it seemed to take forever for my voice to mature. I had a high-pitched voice, and I had come to hate it. Although the high tone had the benefit of allowing me to hit notes on popular songs by Michael Jackson and New Edition, it didn't go over very well in the tough inner-city neighborhood I grew up in. The older guys would tease me, and I would find myself trying to deepen my voice to fit into the machismo and testosterone jungle I was surrounded by. What I didn't know at the time, however, was that the unique voice that I hated would become the distinct sound God would later use to touch and inspire countless lives in the future. Sometimes the thing you wish you could change about yourself is the thing God will use to set you on high.

The key to overcoming negative thoughts and fears about your distinction is to renew your mind daily with truth affirmations about yourself.

Here are some examples of mind-renewing affirmations:

1. **My distinction is the key to my success, significance, and prosperity.**
2. **I'm an epic creation of God Almighty, and no one else can do what I am ordained to do.**
3. **My distinction will work for me, not against me.**
4. **I was born to stand out and shine bright, and I will not shrink to fit in.**
5. **My uniqueness is significant and vital to the world around me.**

Purpose seekers must learn how to encourage themselves. What you meditate on and speak about will help you tremendously. Memorize these affirming truths, and speak them over your life daily. The more you repeat these affirmations, the more you will come to believe in your distinction. This will cause your distinction to rise more and more to the surface. You'll begin to sharpen it and master it until it becomes the very thing that leads your life and defines your path. Your distinction is what makes you remarkable! It's the *It Factor* of your life. It's the only key that unlocks your purpose and your destiny. It's the one thing that is guaranteed to work. Your life maximized is your life lived out in your distinction.

You Are Different to Make a Difference

One thing to understand about your distinction is this—you were made different to make a difference. There is a unique contribution that your life is to make on the society that you were birthed into. When God planned the masterpiece of you, His thoughts went beyond just you, and also factored in the impact your life would make on the world around you. In other words, there is something that this world needs that only your life can supply. If you never embraced your distinction and instead spent your life trying to "fit in," the world would be robbed of the gift that your life offers.

The truth is, your life really isn't about you. It's about everyone your life is meant to touch. Every life is connected to another life. This is even illustrated in biology. Think about it. Every time you see one person, at least three are represented—the mother, the father, and the person you see. I believe that God set it up this way so that even in looking in the mirror there is a constant reminder that our lives are interconnected with others.

The purpose of your life is not for your life, just as a tool doesn't exist to fix itself. Your purpose is connected to people who are in need of you, and your distinction is a perfect match for the things they lack.

Blazing Your Trail

In order to bridge the gap between your purpose and the world that is awaiting it, you will have to become a trailblazer. When we think of a trailblazer our minds may immediately go to distinguished personalities of the past who accomplished great things and changed the world they lived in. These could be innovators in technology, science, entertainment, or culture. Perhaps when we think of trailblazers we consider civil rights leaders like Dr. Martin Luther King Jr. and others whose lives and sacrifices helped shape the society we live in. There are a number of people that come to mind when thinking about trailblazers, yet many people never consider the trailblazer in the mirror. Every single one of us has a trail to blaze. We are all pioneers of our purpose. Breaking out of the pack is about blazing the trail God has preordained for you. It's about being that runner in the race who starts out in the pack, gets his footing, discovers his distinction, finds his own lane, and blazes his trail.

You are a trailblazer. No one else is qualified or called to do what you are specifically designed to do. Everything about your life has been shaped to accomplish a specific function that has never been done before. The trail that you blaze will leave an indelible mark on this world, and because you were in the world, it will never be the same again.

Now that you are officially a trailblazer there are some things you need to know about yourself. Here are five key traits every trailblazer must have:

1. They're not afraid to be the first one

Trailblazers lead the pack. They aren't afraid to be the first to do something—as a matter of fact they expect to be. They acknowledge their unique gifting and sense of purpose and therefore seize every opportunity to make a difference, even if it involves doing the never been seen before.

2. They stay in their lane

Although trailblazers are remarkably convinced of who they are, they are also quite comfortable with knowing who they are not. The strength of the trailblazer is that they know the trail that they are supposed to be on. They believe that investing time in a trail that isn't theirs is detrimental to the one that is. They are focused and intentional, and they can quickly discern between a good lane and a God lane. Trailblazers are disciplined to embrace the God lane only and avoid all others.

3. They don't compare themselves to others

Trailblazers understand the folly in comparing themselves to others. They recognize that there can never be an apples-to-apples comparison between people, because no two people are the same, nor is their purpose or path identical. A comparison to another will always return a false analysis, either causing them to falsely come up short or to be stroked with pride in thinking they are better at purpose than another. The only thing that trailblazers measure themselves by is their faithfulness in blazing the trail that they have been assigned to.

4. They sacrifice for others

Trailblazers realize that they are blazing a trail for others who will follow. They sacrifice and understand that their life is bigger than themselves. They see sacrifice as an investment and know that if they sacrifice their life for others, God will give them their life back with interest. They pursue greatness not for the sake of greatness, but so their life can have a great impact on the lives of others around them. They acknowledge that God's dream for their life trumps their own, and therefore they make God's dream theirs.

5. They're not afraid to be alone

Trailblazers are not afraid to stand alone when the season requires it. They understand that their calling is to pave the way for others, not necessarily to pave the way *with* others. They recognize, most of the time, the crowds will show up after the trail has been blazed. They don't require anyone else to see what they see or stand where they stand in the beginning of a new trail.

In blazing my own trail there have been several times I had to go solo on a new path while others waited, partially committed, until the road was paved. Then once the trail was blazed, they walked on it and rejoiced in its benefits. As a trailblazer, you can't expect people to see what you see in the beginning or feel discouraged if you are left alone on your new trail. The reason why you are called to blaze your own trail is because you are the only one who can. Make sure that you are committed to the trail, and the fruit of your efforts will soon be plainly seen.

It's Time to Break Out

Sometimes I wonder what my life would be like if I had never broken out of the pack. Honestly, the thought is more like a nightmare. Not only would I be unfulfilled and living way beneath my potential, but my impact on society would be significantly reduced. These thoughts are almost too painful to bear, but I allow myself to think of them as a reminder to continue forward.

Do you ever think about what people are going to say about your life when you leave this earth? I've gone to funerals where I have been shocked to find out more about a person's accomplishments at their death than I knew while they were alive. So many people from various stages of the deceased's life get up and share about the person's impact on their life and the difference it made. In a way, it was as if the person was still alive because of all the good they'd done in the world, and because of the people still alive to perpetuate that goodness. When you break out of the pack and discover your distinction, your life will have the same effect.

I want to leave you with a quote from one of the greatest trailblazers in American history, Dr. Martin Luther King Jr. He broke out of the pack of complacency, fear, and the toleration of injustice, and blazed a trail for human rights that many people are still walking on today. Let these words forever be a reminder to you of what life is really about and the difference you have the privilege of making in this world through pursuing God's epic idea for your life.

If any of you are around when I have to meet my day, I don't want a long funeral. And if you get somebody to deliver the eulogy, tell them not to talk too long. And every now and then I wonder what I want them to say. Tell them not to mention that I have a Nobel Peace Prize—that isn't important. Tell them not to mention that I have three or four hundred other awards—that's not important. Tell them not to mention where I went to school.

I'd like somebody to mention that day that Martin Luther King Jr., tried to give his life serving others. I'd like for somebody to say that day that Martin Luther King Jr., tried to love somebody. I want you to say that day that I tried to be right on the war question. I want you to be able to say that day that I did try to feed the hungry. And I want you to be able to say that day that I did try in my life to clothe those who were naked. I want you to say on that day that I did try in my life to visit those who were in prison. I want you to say that I tried to love and serve humanity.

Yes, if you want to say that I was a drum major, say that I was a drum major for justice. Say that I was a drum major for peace. I was a drum major for righteousness. And all of the other shallow things will not matter.

—Dr. Martin Luther King Jr.,
"Drum Major Instinct" sermon, 1968

Part III

FAITH

The Journey Fuel

Chapter 7

PLANES, TRAINS, AND FAITH

The journey of purpose and the pursuing of the epic idea that motivated your birth is one of faith. Faith is what initiates the voyage, sustains the course, completes the mission, and manifests the promise. On your trek to destiny, your faith will be the vehicle, the map, the road, and the destination. In the physical world, the transportation systems include planes, trains, and automobiles. On the path of purpose, however, what moves you along is faith, faith, and more faith. If I haven't made it clear enough yet—you must have faith to live out purpose!

To be honest, I don't know a whole lot of people who start leaping for joy at the thought of having to rely on their faith for something they really need. We are much more comfortable with concrete evidence, information, and proven formulas when it comes down to it. If we had the power to determine the course of our lives, we would make it so we'd never have to trust blindly for anything. I totally get it. Faith is not easy—but the rewards are incomparable.

Let's answer some common questions about faith. Questions like: *What is faith? Where does it come from? How do we get it?* There are five primary things you need to know about faith. When you understand these things, you become empowered to not only discover your purpose, but to walk it out with assurance. We are going to explore these five essentials of faith:

1. What *faith* is.
2. Where *faith* comes from.
3. You have *faith* already.
4. What *faith* means to God.
5. How to apply *faith*.

The Definition of Faith

There is no shortage of the use of the word *faith* in our world today, but does the average person really know what faith means? We see T-shirts, bumper stickers, and key chains, all having the word *faith* on them, but what is faith really? I suppose the answer to that question really depends on who you ask, because faith means different things to different people. For some, faith is associated with spiritual beliefs or religious convictions. Another person will describe faith as inspiration or hope. Some use the term "keep the faith" as encouragement, instructing a person to stay positive or optimistic when going through a difficult time. All of these definitions are valid and true, but the type of faith that leads to purpose and destiny is something more specific and much deeper.

There's a passage in Scripture that defines faith in a way that I had once never considered. It defines faith at the deepest level, and it has revolutionized my thinking and totally transformed my life. Let's look at what it says about faith:

Now faith is the substance of things hoped for, the evidence of things not seen. (Hebrews 11:1)

Wow! There is so much being said here in just a few words. When you get the full understanding of what's being said in this short but comprehensive passage, your life is going to change. This is the revelation about faith your destiny has been waiting for you to grasp. Let's explore this passage deeper.

The first thing that this passage tells us is that faith *has substance*. Faith is not blind, empty, or as uncertain as we may think. It's certainly more than just wishful thinking. Faith has matter. Faith is real and involves real things. The realities of faith aren't based on what you can see—they're based on the guarantee of what you one day will see.

The original word in the passage that was translated "substance" is a Greek word derived from two words. One of the words is *under*. The other word can be translated *established*. When you put the words together you get the idea of something being *established under*. What the passage is saying is that faith is something that exists already, yet for now has only been "established under" in the unseen realm. In the process of time, however, what has been established under will be manifest above, into the seen realm. Here's what I mean:

You buy a home and move into it. When you bought the house you planned on landscaping the backyard, because there seemed to be nothing more than dirt where you wanted to have a garden. But after you move in it rains, and you surprisingly notice beautiful tulips growing in the place where you previously saw nothing. This causes you to realize that just because you couldn't see anything initially didn't mean that something was not there. You just couldn't see it yet. There were tulip bulbs planted in the ground the entire time. They were just *established under*, but at the appointed time what had been unseen became clearly evident.

This is faith. It's understanding that reality isn't one-dimensional. Reality spans across two realms—the seen and the soon to be seen. Faith breaks us out of the limiting belief that only seeing is believing. Natural sight can be very restricting. Sometimes you have to close your eyes in the natural world in order to truly see what *is*.

Faith Comes from God

Let's look again at the passage. It says "faith is the substance of *things hoped for*, the evidence of things not seen." The phrase *things hoped for* comes from one Greek word that contains the word *expectation* at its root. This means that the passage could better be read: "Faith is the substance of *expectation*, the evidence of things not seen." Why do I point out this distinction by drawing attention to the word *expectation*? Because it reveals that real faith must begin with something being promised to the faith-holder. We know this because a promise has to be in place in order to create an expectation. You can't expect something you haven't been assured of.

This means that this type of faith requires a God encounter. When the Almighty God has purposed to do something in your life, He first engages you and tells you what He is going to do. At the point of God revealing to you what He has planned to do, an expectation begins to arise within you. Because the plans of God will never fail, faith becomes your expectation of what is guaranteed to happen. In essence you simply become the birthing channel that manifests what God has already accomplished in the unseen realm.

When God approached our friend Abraham and made him those great promises, He was instilling in Abraham the assurance of what He had already preordained. This assurance is what produced mobility in Abraham, causing him to leave behind his familiar surroundings for a promise that he knew without question had to exist. This expectation of what God had promised had guided and encouraged him at every step of his journey. Abraham, after a lifestyle of faith, witnessed the fulfillment of every promise God had made. True faith, the kind that never disappoints, comes from God.

Everyone Has Faith

One thing that never fails to show up on a person's spiritual wish list is the desire for more faith. People often marvel at others who appear to have great faith, saying, "Wow! I wish I had that type of faith!" Without the right understanding, it's easy to believe that great faith is a rare endowment that only a select few are blessed to have. Some even find it difficult to see themselves as people who could one day live by great faith. Yet there's something very telling about this widespread quest for faith—it suggests that deep down we all know we need it. There is something in us that knows there's more than what our eyes can see. We know inherently that to live by sight alone will restrict us to a single dimension in a world that's multidimensional. We all need faith. The good news is, we all have it.

God has dealt to each one a measure of faith. (see Romans 12:3)

This incredible passage states plainly that God has already given a measure of faith to each one of us. God is a master planner and a profound strategist. He covers all bases and leaves no stone unturned. He knows that faith is a nonnegotiable on your journey to purpose, and therefore He properly prepares each of us by equipping us with it. Faith is not something that God has to put in you—it's already there.

If you really think about it, even the desire *for* faith is a sign of the presence *of* faith. It takes a certain amount of faith to even believe in the existence of more faith. This is the measure of faith God gives all of us to start with. It produces a seeking for more faith, spirituality, and the meaning of life. This seeking is really a search for God. It's all by design. God wants to be found by us and therefore gives us a measure of faith to help facilitate the introduction. Then, once you find Him, He starts to communicate truth and encourages you with His promises. Your initial measure of faith begins to grow because of these promises, which cause you to expect what He says. Next, your faith grows even more as you witness fulfilled promises, and the cycle keeps going.

Great faith doesn't happen overnight, however. It's the by-product of consistently witnessing God fulfilling His promise time and time again. I'm sure you've heard it said before that if you have faith the size of a tiny mustard seed, you can move a mountain. This is true, but it doesn't mean that little faith gets big results. It simply means that all great faith started out as small faith. You've already been given the necessary portion of faith for your journey—you just have to make it grow. As you seek the One who gave you faith, it will grow from just a measure of faith into the type of faith that will turn mountains into molehills.

Your Faith Pleases God

But without faith it is impossible to please Him, for he who comes to God must believe that He is, and that He is a rewarder of those who diligently seek Him. (Hebrews 11:6)

This is another one of my favorite passages in Scripture, but sadly it's sometimes used in a negative way, as opposed to the affirming spirit in which it was intended. Some people misguidedly quote this verse to invoke fear in others by suggesting that if you don't give God what He is looking for, He's not going to be pleased with you. This is so far from the truth. In fact, this passage is actually meant to be very inspiring. Let's dissect it a bit.

It starts with "But without faith it is impossible to please Him." This is where some people get confused because there are two ways to look at this verse. You can read it and be inspired, or you can read it and get discouraged. This verse is not the voice of God telling us it's impossible for any of us to please Him. Instead, He is teaching us about the very thing that does. In a way, it's like God is showing us how to relate to Him so we can grow in intimacy with Him and enjoy the rich benefits of that bond. It's like with any other relationship. The best of them work when people communicate, understand each other, and learn how to relate to one another.

This passage conveys God's heart and His desire to guide you to all He's got planned for you, and to spare you from wasting time trying to impress Him with things that, well, don't.

It's like the guy on the first date trying to impress his lady by getting all gussied up and taking her out to a fancy-schmancy dinner. He stresses himself out and spends a ton of money trying to impress her, only to find out later once he gets to know her, that El Pollo Loco and good conversation would have been enough. Had he known up front what really moved his lady's heart, he would have been spared a lot of hassle, and saved his money.

What the passage relays, rather, is that we've been given the opportunity to please the Almighty God who created the universe. This communicates our significance, value, and profound capabilities. The idea that we, made from the dust of the ground, can invoke joy in our Maker is mind-blowing. What brings Him joy is faith—and you have it. Remember, He gave it to you. You're destined to win because the very thing He requires, you already possess.

The passage continues, "for he who comes to God must believe that He is, and that He is a rewarder of those who diligently seek Him."

If there's one thing I've learned and personally experienced since starting my journey to purpose, it's that God wholeheartedly longs to reward His children. He doesn't reward in the way we might envision. He is not Santa Claus. It's much deeper than us being naughty or nice. It's not about you being good or bad per se—it's about what moves God. Nothing moves Him more than your alignment with His original idea for your life. So basically, God rewards you for being you—the real you. This all ties back to your faith and why it's so important. Your journey to purpose is your journey to discovering the epic idea that motivated your birth. Your faith leads you to the instructions that guide you on the course of your destiny. As we apply these instructions, God rewards us with the blessings His epic plan entails.

The Application of Faith

Now the just shall live by faith. (see Hebrews 10:38)

The journey to discovering purpose requires not only that you have faith, but that it becomes your new lifestyle. Faith becomes a lifestyle when you transition from living only by things that you see to believing in everything that God reveals, even if your natural eyes have not seen it yet. Living by faith is an incredible lifestyle. It's a lifestyle that takes the limits off the sky and allows you to live in a realm where all things are possible.

Living by faith is exciting. I'm not referring to the type of reckless excitement I had—umm (clears throat), I mean some people had, when they were freshmen in college being away from home for the first time. I don't mean carefree, irresponsible excitement that you later have to pay for. I'm talking about the excitement that happens when the possibilities for your life become endless because you've hooked up with the One who hung the stars in outer space. The lifestyle of faith erases the periods we place in our life story and replaces them with commas, question marks, dashes, and exclamation points! When I look at my life today and all that has unfolded, I realize that there isn't one major blessing I received that didn't start as an invisible promise I chose to believe in.

The Good Thing vs. the God Thing

The lifestyle of faith has a cost nevertheless, and I won't kid you—it's not cheap. The cost is sacrifice. In order to live by faith, sometimes you'll have to be willing to sacrifice the thing you see today for the thing God promises to manifest tomorrow. Doing this is never easy. Most people subscribe to the philosophy that a bird in the hand is better than two in the bush. Although I agree that at times this saying may be relevant, in the world of faith it often is not. The road to purpose is full of occasions that require you to sacrifice the *good thing* in order to receive the *God thing*. There *is* a difference. The good thing might be good, but may not be God's best for you. The good thing may be good today, but in six months it can become the bad thing. If this happens, you're forced to go back to square one, after wasting valuable time. The good thing may also appear to be good only because you're not seeing everything needed to sustain your path of purpose. If you opt for the good and it causes you to stray off course, then what you were calling "good" will prove to really have been just a distraction.

The God thing, however, is everything that the good thing promises, and far beyond. The most important fact about the God thing is it will always be aligned with your purpose. It's the route you have to take, even when it hurts. You never want to be sidetracked from purpose because a good thing opened up. Choosing well in moments like this requires patience, but if you hold out for the best it will not disappoint. The God thing often is right on the other side of your patience and self-control. Some of the best decisions I've ever made were when I chose to painstakingly sacrifice the good thing in expectation of the God thing I had been promised.

There was a time when I was interviewing for a job and had narrowed my search down to the top three companies, each of which were suitable. Of the three, however, one stood out to me and fit perfectly into my family and church life. After the final interviewing processes, two of the three companies offered me the position. Guess which one didn't? Yep—the one I really wanted. This third company was still evaluating two of their other top candidates. While I waited for the third company to respond, I was able to delay giving an answer to the other two companies. A week went by and still nothing. Meanwhile, the other two companies held out as long as they could until they finally forced me to either accept their offer or they would hire the next candidate on their list.

This put me in a jam. The job I really wanted—the job that I prayed for, had not made me an offer, and I had two others ready to put me on the payroll. The pressure was on, and I needed to start bringing money into our home because we had basically gone through all of our savings. But after praying to God and asking Him for this job, a greater measure of faith arose within. I became *one* with the idea that the job I wanted was mine and graciously declined the other two positions, leaving me with nothing concrete except for what my faith was expecting. My faith remained strong for the first full week. After the week was up and I still hadn't heard anything, if I am honest, doubt began to come in like clouds before a storm. When you are waiting to hear from a company you know is eager to hire someone, in my mind no news was NOT good news. But I kept the faith and drove the clouds of doubt away from my heart and mind, and right there in the middle of what seemed like an unpromising situation I stood my ground and claimed that job as mine.

After about three weeks my offer letter came in the mail. This was the job that God wanted me to have, and what I later discovered was that many things that involved my purpose were connected to me working there. What would have happened if I chose the good thing over the God thing? What if I had panicked and ran in another direction? I don't even want to think about it. The point is, the lifestyle of faith will never disappoint and will yield a great payout every time.

Faith is a sacrifice, so try to see it as an investment. You invest in something when you expect to get a greater return. Applying your faith to your life will yield the return of purpose discovered and destiny fulfilled. Faith is how you get around on the course of purpose. It means everything to the process of discovering why you were born. God will give you a vision you can believe in, and your faith will set you out on the course to achieve what you were shown. As your journey continues it will be faith in what God instructs you to do along the way that will keep you on the path of purpose. Living the lifestyle of faith in every season on your journey releases God to progressively unfold to you His brilliant plan for your life.

Chapter 8

MAKING THE INVISIBLE VISIBLE

Something that has always intrigued me is the way time zones work around the world. When it's 7:38 a.m. at home in Los Angeles, it's 10:38 a.m. in Washington, DC. At that same time of the day it's 3:38 p.m. in London, and then there are places like Melbourne, Australia, where the time would be 2:38 a.m. the next day. This is fascinating to me. Confusing at times and frustrating when traveling, but fascinating to me nonetheless. Not because I don't understand hemispheres and the other factors that determine time zones. What amazes me is the parallel between the way the World Clock works and the way life works when you are pursuing your purpose.

Everything we see in our natural world reflects things that exist in the spiritual world. The spiritual world doesn't point to our natural world, it's the other way around—the natural world trains us to better understand the spiritual one. God designed it this way on purpose, so everything in creation would point right back to the One who created it. There's even insight to glean from our World Clock. Not only does it help us to understand how the spiritual realm works, but it also reveals to us the role our faith plays in manifesting our destiny. Allow me to explain.

Have you ever heard of a place called Christmas Island? It's part of the remote island nation Kiribati, positioned far out in the Pacific Ocean. There are many fascinating things about Christmas Island, but it's best known for being the place where the New Year reaches first.

Because of Christmas Island's proximity to the International Dateline, midnight on New Year's hits there first, ahead of any other place in the world. Then as the Earth rotates, the New Year travels across all the other time zones, bringing a sequence of celebrations to people all over the world as they eagerly await the time of their countdown. The farthest regions may have to wait longer than others, but without fail, at the specified time, the whole world experiences what has already taken place on Christmas Island. This process helps us understand how life works in purpose. Everything concerning your purpose has already happened beforehand. It's all moving toward you right on schedule and will show up in your life at the appointed time.

Your purpose is not a random arrangement of events that will one day culminate into something awesome. No—your purpose is a brilliantly designed master plan that unfolds right before your eyes. This unfolding process continues until your life expresses every detail of the masterpiece God envisioned before you were born. However, this unfolding process doesn't happen without your involvement. There's a contribution each of us must make toward our destiny. That contribution is faith. Your faith is what activates this unfolding process.

Let's look at another passage describing faith to better understand this point.

> *By faith we understand that the worlds were framed by the word of God, so that the things which are seen were not made of things which are visible. (Hebrews 11:3)*

There are three insights from this passage that will help you understand how your faith works toward the fulfillment of your purpose.

1. Faith Helps You Understand What Sight Makes You Question

This passage starts off with the words "By faith we understand." That's exactly what faith is designed to do—to bring greater understanding. There is so much about our world we don't understand, and rightly so. After all, it's not like any of us were actually around when the universe was formed. The purpose of faith is not to invoke questioning or doubts—it's to give us revelation. Faith is an amazing gift from God that allows you to peer into a realm beyond your own understanding. Faith causes you to perceive things that without it, you simply couldn't.

Did you know that you have two separate sets of eyes? We know about the ones on our face that allow us to see what's in front of us, but we have another set of eyes called "the eyes of our understanding." These are your spiritual eyes. They allow you to see things not yet visible and give you knowledge of things you never learned. The only thing about these eyes is that they have to be enlightened. In a way, they are similar to candles. I hardly ever notice candles around my home until the power goes out and I need them. These once-neglected candles not only pierce through the darkness giving us much-needed light, but also add a special ambience and warmth to our environment. Although the candles were always there, their value wasn't fully recognized until a situation arose that required their lighting. It's the same with the eyes of your understanding. You are born with them, but just as the candles needed to be lit in order for their benefit to be experienced, the eyes of your understanding have to be awakened so you can clearly see your path to purpose. Gratefully, as we learned in the last chapter, we've each been given a measure of faith, and one of its functions is to turn on your spiritual eyes.

2. The Word Created the Worlds

The passage continues with the phrase "the worlds were framed by the word of God."

This is an amazing reality to ponder. The passage reveals that everything that makes up the vast and unsearchable universe—the Earth, the solar system, every galaxy and the infinite depths of space, were all framed by God's specific instruction. This also means that everything else—including you and me and all the details of our purpose—has been fully accounted for from the beginning of time when God said, "Let there be…" The Greek word that was translated *framed* in the passage means "to complete thoroughly." This tells us that at the very moment God instructed the worlds to be formed, it instantaneously came to be.

This means that the idea of God sitting behind a big desk in heaven managing the universe like a CEO is a fallacy. The truth is, God exists beyond the heavens and simply watches the unfolding of what He commanded from the beginning.

Check out these passages that drive this point home:

> *"I am God, and there is none like me. I make known the end from the beginning, from ancient times, what is still to come. I say, 'My purpose will stand, and I will do all that I please.'" (see Isaiah 46:9–10 NIV)*
>
> *"See, the former things have taken place, and new things I declare; before they spring into being I announce them to you." (Isaiah 42:9 NIV)*

These passages bring us into the mind of God. As you can see, everything God has commanded has already been done. Knowing the way God thinks helps us to understand how He works. This way we know how to partner with Him in realizing our purpose. His ways are so different from ours. When you and I want to accomplish something, we set goals, work hard at it, overcome challenges, and one day see the fruits of our labor. God's way is completely different. All He has to do is desire a thing and it instantaneously becomes reality. There's no working for it, no negotiations, no wishful thinking—it just is. The moment He thinks it and says so, it's done.

Allow this to be a huge encouragement to you as you travel your road to purpose. This means that everything you'll ever need in any situation has already been taken care of. The tab has been picked up and heaven has already bankrolled your future. From the necessary connections to nods needed; from finances to knowledge and information—whatever you need has already been factored in and accounted for, from the beginning of the world. All you have to do is learn to manifest into the visible world, what God has already established in the invisible one.

3. The Invisible Reality

By faith we understand that the worlds were framed by the word of God, so that the things which are seen were not made of things which are visible. (Hebrews 11:3)

Take a moment wherever you are and look around you right now. Take inventory of what you see. You might be seeing chairs, maybe people, cell phones, cars, artwork, trees, or an endless amount of things. No matter what you are looking at, there's something they all have in common: each started off invisible. The house you live in, the car you drive, the clothes you wear, even the meal you prepared started out as nothing more than a plan.

In order to live out the purpose of your life you must learn how to bring the invisible plans that are assigned to your life into the visible world.

Now don't get lost here. Although this process isn't always easy, you can definitely do it. As a matter of fact, you were designed to make this happen over and over again throughout your entire lifetime. Here's an analogy that will help you understand this process.

Any time you see a car, what you are really looking at is something that started off as invisible. To understand how the car came to be, you have to look at its origin. The car didn't start at the car dealership. It didn't start at the manufacturing plant. It didn't even start as an engineering drawing on a computer screen—it began as an idea in someone's mind.

What happened next was that someone had faith in that idea and believed it was possible. That faith motivated them to follow the instructions of the idea, offering their time, talents, and skills to make it a reality. In the process of time, what was invisible becomes visible and someone is driving down the street with the coveted new-car smell. The important thing to realize is that the car actually existed when the thought arose. It just needed faith to manifest it into the visible world. Everything seen came from things that are not seen.

The process works no differently when it comes to manifesting the destiny that God has for you. It's about discovering the plan, having faith in it, moving toward it, and taking action to bring it to pass.

The Plan Is Always Hidden in Plain Sight

"For I know the plans I have for you, plans to prosper you and not to harm you. To give you a future and a hope."

—*God*

There is no one who wants to see the plan for your life materialize more than God. After all, it was His idea from the start. God has a dream concerning you and is committed to seeing it come to fruition. As a result, He is fully devoted to making sure that first of all, you have some idea of what the plan is. He will reveal it to you at the right time, through an inner voice, perhaps a book, the Bible, a spiritual leader, or a friend. Heck—He'll even use a bumper sticker to speak to you. God will use anything He knows will get your attention to reveal to you His plans for your life. Many times God will start revealing His plans to us long before we have any idea what's going on.

When I was a young boy I wanted to be a children's psychologist. This desire stuck with me so long that when I was a freshman in college, it was the major I initially declared. God put that desire in my heart as a clue to what His big plan for me would be. Today, I'm not only counseling and renewing the minds of scores of His *children* but I'm also leading them on a spiritual path and helping them to discover their purpose. God will always make sure that when the time is right you'll know what to do. He's *for* you, and isn't trying to keep you in the dark. He longs to show you His plan. If He never revealed it to you, you could never apply your faith, which is the only way to bring it into the visible world.

Believing Is Everything

There is little that pleases God more than when His children believe in Him. Now—don't take this the wrong way. I'm not suggesting that God sits pouting in heaven with low self-esteem wishing someone would believe in Him. It's not like He needs our affirmation. That's not it at all. He is pleased, however, when we trust Him because He knows our purpose will require our belief. We have to believe Him and follow Him as He leads us forward into the realization of His dream for our lives.

I still get amazed when looking back on a particular time when God gave me a vision of things He wanted to accomplish through my life. The things He showed me then painted the picture of a world to me that was completely different from what my present surroundings were. When I think about it today, what God showed me was pretty outlandish at the time. What He showed me was that I would lead a fresh new multicultural movement focused on authentic spirituality and intimacy with God. He gave me a vision of myself placing an emphasis on teaching, as opposed to preaching, while guiding a generation into spiritual maturity. The only thing was, at the time I was an inexperienced junior-level minister with few responsibilities in a predominately African American church that focused on preaching the basics of spirituality. The reality I stood in was the exact opposite of the vision that God had given. What do you do in moments like that? When something is revealed to you that is so different from not only where you are, but from anything you've ever seen before? And to make matters worse, what do you do when *you* are the one being called upon to bring this impossible vision into reality? I'll tell you what you do. You believe it.

Our good friend Abraham from earlier found himself in a similar situation on his journey to purpose. God made him a promise that he and his wife, Sarah, would have a son who would start an incredible legacy. The only problem was that Sarah had no kids, nor could she, because she was barren. To make matters worse, they were both above the age of bearing children. They were each at least seventy-five years old, if not older, and let's just say they weren't as spry and frisky as they may have been in the good old days. But clearly in God's mind their present situation was totally irrelevant to what He envisioned. God is not limited by circumstance—He's the Creator. He specializes in making something out of nothing. He declares the end of something right from the start because He can.

When He sees you, He sees a finished product and can't help but relate to you accordingly. In other words, God doesn't define you by where you are or by your current circumstance. He deals with you according to what He foreknew about you. Understanding this will help you to believe Him for your future He's promising when the time comes in which you must.

Let's look at the encounter between God and Abraham and learn a few things:

After this, the word of the LORD came to Abram in a vision:
"Do not be afraid, Abram. I am your shield, your very great
reward."

But Abram said, "Sovereign LORD, what can you give me since
I remain childless and the one who will inherit my estate is Eliezer
of Damascus?" And Abram said, "You have given me no children;
so a servant in my household will be my heir."

Then the word of the LORD came to him: "This man will not
be your heir, but a son who is your own flesh and blood will be
your heir." He took him outside and said, "Look up at the sky and
count the stars—if indeed you can count them." Then he said to
him, "So shall your offspring be."

Abram believed the LORD, and he credited it to him as right-
eousness. (Genesis 15:1–6 NIV)

Abraham's story is the perfect example of the process we all must master as we pursue God's purpose for our lives. It began with God approaching Abraham and making him a great promise. Abraham's challenge, however, was that what God was promising looked completely different from what his present reality was. This is a difficult place for a person to be. People are inclined to predict their future based on where they are or perhaps where they have been. Many times this mind-set restricts people and limits them to less than the best that life has to offer. Your future is not based upon what has been nor is it based upon what is. It's based on the things that God has predetermined will be.

In the passage Abraham is questioning what God had promised him because of his current situation so God decides to take him outside and educate him. God invites Abraham to a little lesson in astronomy by asking him to look at the sky and see if he could number the stars. Okay—maybe I embellished a little. God is not giving Abraham a lesson in astronomy. He is giving him a lesson in God-ology. God-ology is the study of God's ability and teaches us that God is great enough to do whatever He purposes, when He wants to, and how He wants to. By showing Abraham the sky and stars, He is basically asking Abraham this:

"Can you explain how these miracles in the sky called stars came to be? Can you explain not only how they got there, but how they remain there forever? No? Okay. Well, let me help you out with that. That would be Me. That's right—I did that. And I didn't just do it once as a fluke. I did it over and over again. I did it so many times that neither you, nor anyone who will come after you, will be able to count all of them. So, Abraham, back to this whole question about whether or not I can give you a son? I kind of feel like you already know what the answer is."

The rest was history. As God reveals His credentials to him, Abraham logically surrenders his concerns and believes in the One who promises. He realizes that it's not his job to understand how God is going to do it. He just needs to know that God can do it, and will.

It's the same for you. You don't need to have all of the answers concerning the awesome things God wants to do, both in and through your life. You just need to believe that He is credible and more than able to bring His promises to pass; even when it's completely different from what you have always known.

At this point, you probably don't need me to tell you the outcome of my own "impossible" situation. You guessed right. I believed God, and the rest was history. I started the movement and it has become a vibrant church that's fulfilling every vision I was given from the start. In the process of time, everything God spoke and even more was manifest into my life.

True Faith and Action Are Inseparable

Belief has evidence and that evidence is action. When you believe that something is so, you take steps to see it fulfilled. In the case of

Abraham, there came a point when he had to go and be intimate with his wife in order to manifest the promise. In the same way (well maybe not in the *exact* same way), I had to take the practical steps toward fulfilling the vision that God gave me. God's word to us sets the miracle in motion, but it's our faith and action that bring the promise to birth.

> *Now faith is the substance of things hoped for, the evidence of things not seen.*

There is a profound insight about faith hidden in this passage. It speaks of a certain type of faith that is more than just believing in something. It describes faith itself *as* the thing we are believing for. Now stay with me here. It says faith *is* the substance of what we are hoping for. Our faith *is* the evidence of what we can't yet see. Here's what this means.

When God speaks a word to us about our future, what He's really doing is revealing to us what actually already exists in the unseen realm. At the moment He speaks it to us, and we believe it, a process is initiated to bring what once was invisible into the seen world. It's like a pregnancy. The process starts off with an announcement that you are going to have a baby. This usually comes from a doctor through a test, long before an ultrasound validates it. At that very moment the now-expecting mother has no more doubts about whether or not she is pregnant. Her reality is that she has substance growing inside of her, although she hasn't even heard the heartbeat.

She begins to alter her life in joyful expectation because of what she knows is growing inside of her. She makes plans for the coming miracle, changes her diet, and modifies her physical activity. She prepares a space in her home and lets the world know that she's expecting a baby. Everything about her life now revolves around the miracle that will soon be manifest for all to see.

It's the same for you when you believe in the miracle that God has promised. By faith you have the promise already, and as you take action and live like it's already so, you too will be able to bring it to pass. You will speak about it like it already is. You will meditate on it, thus causing the creativity that will bring it to pass to flow freely. You won't allow the naysayers to discourage you because in your mind it has already happened. Your faith in whatever God tells you will be the very thing that brings it to birth. True faith inspires movement toward manifesting what's being hoped for. This type of action will bring the promise to fruition every single time.

Making the invisible visible is about partnering with God to unfold what He foreordained for your life. As you believe Him and walk out the instructions to the promise, it manifests the unfolding of His plan. Always remember, it's your faith that sets in motion this unfolding. The invisible realm is where all of the good plans that God has for you exist. You've been empowered through faith to manifest the invisible into your visible world. In the process of time, you will see everything God has in store for you fulfilled right before your eyes.

Chapter 9

TAKING THE LEAP OF FAITH

On your journey to purpose there'll be times when you'll have to take a leap of faith to reach the next chapter of God's plan for your life. Purpose is always progressive and moving forward, but there will be certain times when a major action is needed to maintain your momentum. In those moments there'll be a bridge to cross, and once you do, you'll enter into a greater dimension of your purpose—one you didn't even know existed. A dimension you never would have been able to see, had you remained on the other side of the bridge. Your purpose is always bigger than what you think. This is why God unfolds it to you gradually. If He gave it to us all at once, we'd likely reject it, disqualifying ourselves from accomplishing greatness so far beyond ourselves. God knows our faith capacity at every moment, in every season. Although He stretches our faith, He doesn't do so beyond our ability to remain inspired, and to take action toward the next great thing on our path to fulfilling our purpose.

Remember, God is for you. He's on your side. He's designed your life to be a victorious one. Anything He asks of you, no matter how difficult, He already knows you have the ability to pull off. God never challenges you beyond your ability. The truth is—He challenges you *according* to it. He made you and knows what you can handle in every phase of your life. When the time arrives for you to take a huge step of faith, it's because God has already prequalified you to pass that test.

Taking the leap of faith forward on your road to purpose is a journey within itself. It's never an easy thing to do, but over time you start to get used to it. I've actually gotten pretty good at knowing the cycles and can often sense when a huge faith bridge is lurking. It's usually when I've gotten pretty comfortable in a situation that the last leap of faith brought me into. When things start getting easy and routine I think to myself, "Oh boy. Here we go again." And lo and behold, the next thing I know—I'm on that darn bridge again. I'll admit, when you are in mid-leap it's awkward and uncomfortable, but it's the only way to get to the next phase in your purpose. Without leaps of faith we get sort of lost in a time warp, and the excitement we once had about life and our destiny begins to wane. God wants us to continue to thrive, grow, and prosper in life, and these "faith leaps" are one of the ways He ensures we do.

Never Get Too Comfortable

Two years after starting our church and after finally settling into a regular meeting space, I started feeling like change was on the horizon. We'd gotten pretty comfortable at our location after spending months not knowing where we would meet from week to week. When we first started, we'd meet anyplace that would have us. We met at parks, restaurants, and hotel meeting rooms—once even meeting in the lobby of a hotel. That was a little weird, but hey— when you're first starting out you've got to do what you've got to do, right? But now we had a regular meeting place. We had made it to the big leagues. We could even print flyers with a permanent address on it—hallelujah! We were official. But after the excitement of the move wore off we seemed to settle into a routine. And to be honest, we stopped progressing. It became the same people showing up week after week, we'd do the same thing over and over again, and the church just couldn't seem to grow past a certain point. We were stuck. Although good things were still happening, I knew deep down that something needed to change.

Have you ever had a vision of where you wanted to get to but felt blocked and couldn't figure out how to get there? In those moments, you feel like you're doing all that you know to do, but you're still stuck in a place that you know will never become the place you're envisioning. This could be in a job or in a relationship. It could be in a social group you are a part of or in any number of other scenarios. What I'm describing is something more commonly known as a *dead end*. It's when something isn't going anywhere and deep down you know it. Even the route to purpose will sometimes lead you into what appears to be a dead end. The only thing is, on your road to purpose what looks like a dead end is really an opportunity to take a leap of faith into the next chapter of your destiny.

This is where I was. The church had hit a wall, and I knew it. There was only one thing to do now. I had to ask God one of the bravest questions anyone can ever ask Him—"Lord, what's next?" It takes courage to ask God this question because when you are pursuing your purpose, God's answer to that question will always require some step of faith toward the next plateau He wants to take your life to.

So I asked Him, and He answered me back. His answer was clear. I was to uproot the church from where we were in the city and plant it in a new community in the Valley, way on the other side of town in an area that most of us weren't familiar with. And of course, then there was a voice in my mind taunting me, saying, "See! I told you not to ask!"

God's reply to me was insane! You mean to tell me after we'd finally found a place of consistency, God was telling us to pack our bags and become transients again? Well—as it turned out—this was exactly what God was suggesting that we do. So I did what every other courageous, faith-filled leader would do—I pretended like I couldn't make out what God was saying. Although I had built a ministry on hearing His voice and sharing His word with people, somehow my "spiritual antenna" was "malfunctioning" that day and I couldn't make out those instructions. The funny thing is I actually thought I'd be able to get away with that. Not for long. I dragged my feet for three whole months until finally I was overwhelmed by the nagging reality that things would never progress until I acted on what I heard. I surrendered my opinion on how horrible an idea this would be and decided to trust the omniscient God who held my future in His hands. I finally said yes to His instruction.

For me to say yes was the easy part. Now I had to go convince the congregation to take the plunge with me. I told you a little about how this played out in a previous chapter, but here's the whole story. I'll never forget that Sunday. After I purposely preached a message about stepping out on faith, I dropped the news on my congregation about my plan to move. The sermon went well, but my announcement...let's just say didn't draw thunderous applause. It was a challenging time for me, but you know what? It was just one of those moments when, as a leader pursuing purpose, I just had to be decisive about what I knew God told me. It was settled and we were moving, but there would be more lessons to learn.

The Bridge of Faith

In order to understand the concept of a bridge of faith, you have to think closely about the words. A bridge is something that gets you from one side of a thing to another. It often separates cities and regions. Sometimes the bridge even separates one country from another. Bridges usually take the traveler over a body of water or a steep mountainous terrain. In these instances the bridge is the only way to get to the other side. When we're referring to a bridge of faith, we are referring to a bridge that is invisible. Remember, faith is the substance of things hoped for, the evidence of things *not seen*. Imagine you were traveling across the country, the road that you are traveling on ends, and you come upon a body of water. You can see the road resume in the distance across the water, but there seems to be no road to get you there. This would be quite a predicament for you, and chances are you would turn around, and rightly so.

On the road to purpose, however, things are different. There *is* no turning back. If pursuing purpose seems to lead you to a dead end, it really isn't dead at all. It just means the time has come to travel on the bridge of faith. This bridge will carry you across the wide gulf between where you presently are and where you envision going. The bridge of faith allows you to keep going despite what seems to be lacking and brings you over to the other side into new territories where your promotion and life upgrade exist. The bridge of faith is invisible, but it is a real bridge and is structurally sound enough to fully support you and carry you into the next season of your life.

Let's look at a story in Scripture where Peter, one of Jesus' disciples, stepped out on the bridge of faith and experienced a dimension of living I'm sure he never forgot. It's a story when Peter and his companions needed to go to other side of a region. What he didn't realize is that the other side they were going to wasn't a city like they first thought. It was to the other side of their faith and their understanding that with God all things are possible. Let's peek into the story:

> *Immediately Jesus made His disciples get into the boat and go before Him to the other side, while He sent the multitudes away. But the boat was now in the middle of the sea, tossed by the waves, for the wind was contrary.*
>
> *Now in the fourth watch of the night Jesus went to them, walking on the sea. And when the disciples saw Him walking on the sea, they were troubled, saying, "It is a ghost!" And they cried out for fear.*
>
> *But immediately Jesus spoke to them, saying, "Be of good cheer! It is I; do not be afraid."*

And Peter answered Him and said, "Lord, if it is You, command me to come to You on the water."

So He said, "Come." And when Peter had come down out of the boat, he walked on the water to go to Jesus. But when he saw that the wind was boisterous, he was afraid; and beginning to sink he cried out, saying, "Lord, save me!"

And immediately Jesus stretched out His hand and caught him, and said to him, "O you of little faith, why did you doubt?" And when they got into the boat, the wind ceased. (Matthew 14:22–32)

What an incredible story filled with so many truths and lessons we can apply to our lives, especially when we find ourselves in moments that require leaps of faith. This story was totally staged by God to bring the disciples of Jesus to a place of understanding about how their faith could manifest things that seem impossible.

The story begins with the disciples in a boat trying to get to the "other side" of a lake. A violent storm comes and begins to toss the boat around on the water. The disciples begin to panic. Not only were they afraid of being capsized, but they also became gripped by fear when they saw Jesus coming toward them walking on water, assuming He was a ghost. To keep them from dying of heart failure, Jesus calls out from the sea and assures them that He's not a ghost. Peter, one of the disciples, calls to Jesus and says, "If it's really you, allow me to walk on the water to you." What happens next is incredible!

Just moments before Peter calls out to Jesus in a way that took great faith, he was part of the group on the boat that had been overcome by great fear. What a major mood swing! This lets me know that there's a thin line between fear and faith. Think about it. Fear is an overwhelming energy that locks you into the belief of a particular outcome. Fear is actually faith—just in the wrong thing. I believe the reason Peter could so quickly switch from fear to faith was because the difference was only a matter of what he locked his eyes on.

None of the others make the request that Peter does, because their eyes were still locked on the storm.

Peter chooses instead to lock his eyes on Jesus who was walking toward them. In an instant, he goes from being consumed with great fear to being possessed with great faith and the rest was history—literally. Before Peter's brain could catch up with his mouth, his faith-filled heart asks Jesus if he could walk on the water to Him.

This is what happens when you make God your focus and not your surroundings. Your imagination gets unlocked and you begin to consider possibilities that have never been done before. Your purpose and destiny requires your imagination. There are visions and dreams hidden in the recesses of your mind that rise to the surface when you meditate on God's amazingness. As Peter saw Jesus doing the impossible, he immediately identified with his own ability for greatness. He asks Jesus to allow him to do the impossible, and Jesus affirms him with one word—"Come!"

Before Peter had time to think, he was out of the boat and feeling a sensation he had never experienced before. The sea underneath his feet, for the first time, felt like solid ground. Peter was now walking on water. He stepped out into what looked like nothing and discovered quickly it was more than he could have asked for. This was Peter's bridge of faith, and it took him from ordinary to extraordinary in an instant, simply by his willingness to cross it.

God's the Architect of the Bridge of Faith

There's one last thing you need to know about the bridge of faith. It's a very critical insight found in the water-walking story. This insight explains how bridges of faith are created. If you recall in the story, Peter doesn't get out of the boat before asking if Jesus would allow it. This leads to a critical truth, so let me be direct. A bridge of faith is not an imaginary structure based solely on what we want or what we randomly claim at any second. There are no guarantees in those instances. If Peter had just gotten excited and hopped out of the boat, the story would have ended much differently. It likely would have involved the other disciples tossing some sort of life preserver into the sea to save Peter's overly ambitious life. Although later in the story Peter begins to sink after being distracted, the fact remains that he did the impossible—he walked on water, and there is a reason why he could. His ability to walk on water was the result of one simple word that Jesus gave him. It's when He answered Peter and said the word "Come!" This was not simply a word of encouragement that Jesus was giving to Peter. This word had power and was loaded with all of the resources necessary to allow Peter to do what he envisioned. That word *come* would cause the entire universe to align in such a way that it had to produce the very thing that the Lord had approved. In essence, Peter had to walk on water because Jesus said so. In fact, the truth is, Peter didn't really walk on the water—he walked on the word God spoke. Remember—*the worlds were framed by the word of God.*

Every bridge of faith you'll have to cross has already been built for you in the unseen realm. The key is to ask God for permission to cross it without being distracted by the appearance of what seems to be missing. All you need to know is whether God said so or not. If He has, rest assured it's already done. This means the bridge has been built and is in place, just waiting to be traveled on. All you have to do is cross it.

You Know It's God If It Requires God

After telling the congregation that we were moving, it was time to find a place. During my season of feet dragging, I'd put mild feelers out to see what type of properties could be our new home. Interestingly, nothing came up while I was only partially committed. It was as if God were saying, "Look, man, I don't have time for games. If you are serious, miracles await you, if not, you can go around this mountain all by yourself." The moment I committed in my heart to move, the very same day, I got a *random* call telling me the perfect location for our church had been found. It was also in the exact neighborhood God had spoken to me about. My wife and I rushed to see it that day, and it was more perfect in person than what we had been told over the phone.

When you are aligned with God in your heart and actions, it puts you on the fast track of what He is doing. Here's the reality—if He's doing it, it's already done. Getting with His program allows us to catch up with what has already been established, waiting for us to discover it.

The new building was beautiful. It was more than what we needed or had hoped to secure. There were classrooms for the children and it had great sound and media equipment. Everything about it was perfect, but there was one major setback—it was way out of our price range. The minimum bid they were accepting was more than twice our current budget, and there were several other groups bidding at the same time. In that moment, I had a decision to make. I could choose to say, "Well, I guess God has something else for me," or I could be still, keep my eye on God, and listen intently for Him to say, "Come."

In the natural world I was way out of my league, but there was something within that assured me this property was mine. It was my faith talking to me. You see, real faith is not moved by mountains—real faith moves mountains. I turned up the volume of my faith and put the voice of fear and doubt on mute. It was awesome! Right there on the spot we made an offer. Now watch this—we didn't make an offer based on what we had—we made the offer based on what we were trusting God would provide. My wife and I walked away with confidence, leaving it completely in God's hands.

Time went by and we didn't hear any news. This is when I learned that faith has to be exercised. It's like a muscle, and if it isn't put to use it will either be lost or not as robust as it should be. You've got to understand something. When you give something to God, it doesn't mean you pray once, turn it over to Him, and never think about it anymore. That's not faith. At times, that could be more of a doubt pattern than a pattern of faith. Giving a situation that you are hoping for to God is about trusting that God can bring it to pass. Your faith is still involved, and you live with a constant and continuous expectation of the manifestation of what you are hoping for.

I had to work my faith. I would drive over to the new building, walk around it, lay my hands on it, and claim it as ours. I would make sure I looked at that building every single day. Each time I saw it, my faith grew larger. Big miracles require big faith. If you are in a situation that requires a big miracle but you don't feel like you have big faith, don't be alarmed. It can grow. Just take the faith that you have and start working it. Do not allow thoughts of fear and doubt to hang out in your mind, but rather choose to meditate on the outcome you're looking for. It doesn't cost you anything to believe for what you want, but not believing could cost you everything. Remember, your faith is what brings the thing to pass. Go back over the steps that got you to this point. Remember all of the confirmation you received. Those were God's reassurances to you that He will bring the miracle to pass. Sometimes God will frontload you with confirmations because He knows a season is coming that will test your faith. He wants you to remember all of the promises and reassurances He made to you from the beginning and wants you to know there's no circumstance great enough to make His promises void. There is nothing too hard for God to do.

Thrust into the Deep

Leaps of faith aren't always fun, but all of them turn out amazing! Sometimes you'll even get forced into an unexpected leap of faith. At times God has to help us along in the plan He has for us because of our tendency to remain in comfortable situations. Believe me, I know all about that. I guess it doesn't really matter how you get to your next level as long as you get there. Whether you take the plunge or get thrown into the deep, the outcome will be the same—an upgrade in your life.

I'm sure you know what the end of our story was. That's right! God did it again. The owners contacted us and honored our bid. The property was ours. We had no doubt it was God's reward to us for our steadfast position of unwavering faith. I'm fully convinced that had we not contended for the property with our faith, it would have gone to someone else—perhaps someone who had the type of faith that pleases Him.

Your faith is the substance of what you are hoping for, the evidence of what you cannot see. Evidence is something that proves to a judge that you are legitimate in causing him to decide in your favor. It's the same with God. When He looks and sees your faith, you prove to Him that you already have the thing He is longing to give you. From there it's just a matter of timing, and what you've expected will be manifest.

Oh, I almost forgot something. A donor in our church unexpectedly came into a large sum of money and made a significant contribution that covered the relocation. Also, our budget grew overnight, causing us to never feel a financial burden even though we started paying twice as much as we had before. God had it all worked out. Leaps of faith always start off in the red, but when God shows up it always proves to be more than enough. When He said to us, "Come," He was in essence saying,

> *"Come and see what I have already prepared for you. I've gone ahead of you and worked out all of the details. The other side is waiting for you to inhabit it. I've prepared a space for you in the next chapter of the Book of You. Take a leap of faith, turn the page; your destiny awaits you."*

Every major upgrade on your journey to purpose will require a radical act of faith. These periodic leaps are how God gets you from where you are to where He already sees you standing. Don't be alarmed if what He is promising seems bigger than you—that's normal. It wouldn't be a God thing if you didn't need *Him* to pull it off. All you need is His word, "Come." When He gives it to you, you're empowered to do whatever that word says. Everything you need to get from where you are to where you are going is contained in that instruction. The bridge of faith will carry you over from one chapter of your story to the next. As you make these leaps a lifestyle, you will be unstoppable in fulfilling the epic idea that motivated your birth.

Part IV

BECOMING YOU

Chapter 10

THE DEFINITION OF (W)HOL(E)Y

The further you get on your journey in purpose, the more you begin to realize just how "into you" God really is. He has a way of making every one of us feel like His favorite. And the truth is—we all are. God didn't make us in groups. He fashioned each one of us individually. He wasn't thinking about anyone else when He dreamed of your life, called it epic, and made you. You *are* His favorite one. This is what makes God like no other. He can give Himself entirely and exclusively to each one of us, all at the same time, and that's exactly what He does.

There's a place in Scripture where God calls Himself a jealous God. Some misinterpret what this means. It doesn't suggest that God is filled with envy when we put our trust in other things. That's not it at all. It doesn't mean that God is jealous *of* us or *about* us—it means that God is jealous *for* us. He wants us. His passion is to show us why we should want Him too. God loves us endlessly and knows that no one or nothing on the planet has the capacity to love us at the level in which He does. Think about it. Who could love you better than the One who loved you before you were ever born? Who could love you more than the One who knows every hidden thing about you, down to your thoughts, and still loves you all the more? Who meditates on you day and night, and delights in you just the way you are? Who loves the things about you that others make fun of or take for granted? Who sees the beauty in every part of you, even when you don't see it in yourself? I could go on and on, but let me state plainly—the answer is no one but our amazing God. He knows this about Himself and therefore is jealous *for* you.

One thing that amazes me about God is how much of a giver He is, yet He wants nothing in return. Where do you find someone who only wants *for* you—not *from* you? Many times a person's goodness is extended toward you because of what they feel they can get from you. This type of kindness comes with an agenda, which ultimately boils down to selfishness. But with God it's the exact opposite. His kindness is simply because He's kind, and His goodness because He's good. He couldn't be anything else if He tried. It's His nature. This kind of love is impossible to find, yet the Creator of the world freely gives it to each of us. Sometimes I try to find a reason for the existence of God other than to bless us children, and I have yet to find it. He lives to sustain and prosper the very best thing He's ever made— His children, who have been created in His image.

There's a passage that captures God's heart and intentions for us so perfectly that it's become the very foundation of my relationship with Him. It dispels all of the false ideas about God and demystifies what His true motivations are concerning us. Because of what this passage clearly communicates, I've come to trust God with my entire life. We read it earlier, but in case you missed it—here it is again:

"For I know the plans I have for you," says the LORD, "plans to prosper you and not to harm you, to give you a future and a hope." (Jeremiah 29:11 NIV)

This is God's heart for His creation made plain and simple. He wants to prosper us. If you listen closely, you can hear God's reassuring voice telling us He's fully aware of the *idea* He has for us. After all, it's the only thing He envisions when He thinks of us. Think about that for a second. God doesn't define us by our present or by who we think we are. He sees us in completion. In other words, all He can see when He looks at us is the finished product. He then encourages us in ways that move us toward what he is envisioning.

In this passage, a word is used that was translated "prosper." Although prosper is a good translation of the original word, the better translation of that word is "to be completed" or "to be complete." Both of these meanings are implied in what God is saying.

First, He is guaranteeing that the things He plans for us, He will complete. He is also saying that not only will His plans be completed, He will make *us* complete in the process. God is saying on one hand that your better days are not behind you but in front of you. When He speaks in the passage about the future He's giving you, He's talking about the realization of His epic plan for you. In essence, He's saying that His plan is in full effect. Sometimes we have to be reminded of this when we are in a season that causes us to question if what we've been hoping for will ever show up. Life will sometimes take an unexpected turn that makes you wonder if the good plans for your destiny have been scrapped. The answer to that question will always be, "No."

God is not a God of many foundations but only a few buildings. He completes what He starts. As a matter of fact, it was finished before it even began. When God says that He will prosper you, one of the things He's promising is to bring to completion the thing He started with you before you were born. In purpose, your best days are always in front of you.

The word *prosper* in the passage also has another meaning. It means for us to be complete or to be made whole. It's this definition in particular that I'd really like for us to dig into.

Who Really Wants to Be Holy Anyway?

I've got a question for you, and I want you to be honest. What does the word *holy* mean to you? Take a second and think about it. I had an idea of what most people thought, but wanted to see if my suspicions were true. I decided to conduct my own scientific and "very official survey" on the subject, so I went to the go-to source for current information and popular opinion. You guessed it—Twitter. Almost immediately after sending out the tweet about the word *holy*, I started getting some interesting replies, most of which confirmed what I felt the general consensus would be. Some of the replies I received included: untouchable, unreachable, judgmental, overly honest, purity, square, swagless, righteous, overly religious, reverence, apart from the rest, above and beyond, higher, without sin, sacrifice, high and mighty.

My suspicions were true. The majority of people associated the word *holy* either with a negative connotation or in a way that suggested that only the "pure" are worthy of approaching or attaining it. But there's a problem here—none of these definitions or attributes given to the word *holy* are accurate. Holy literally means "to be whole." It doesn't even mean sacred like many people think. That's a connotation that was given to it, but the root of the word means whole. Holy means to be perfectly complete and spiritually whole.

So the question becomes, how did the term holy come to be seen as untouchable, overly religious, unreachable, and judgmental? The answer is simple. It has to do with some people's interpretation of God and how *they* have presented Him to others. According to some people's commentary about Him, He is unapproachable, condemning, standoffish, selective, and just one bad report away from sending all of us to hell. What further complicates things is when people call *themselves* holy, but then appear self-righteous, overly critical, holier than thou, and, at times, flat-out obnoxious. When you have a society that has been conditioned to think this way about God for centuries, and people who take ownership of the term and project a loveless image, there is no question why the term *holy* has become so controversial.

So in a sense, this key attribute of God has been hijacked from Him, and as a result, the very thing designed to draw people to Him has now become the thing that pushes people away. This has to be something that grieves God deeply. I say it all of the time and here it is again—God's got the worst PR ever. I don't say that to be critical. I'm just acknowledging the shortcomings we all have and our tendency to project onto God characteristics that are far from who He truly is. He is holy, meaning He is whole in every way and wants nothing more than to have His children be spiritually whole as well.

Holy Isn't a Behavior, It's a Becoming

Because it is written, "Be holy, for I am holy." (1 Peter 1:16)

There are several passages of Scripture where God calls his children to be holy. I think it's important to note what God is NOT saying in these passages. God is not associating being holy with behavior. To see holiness in this way is a huge mistake. To be holy is about becoming—not doing. God is more interested in you *becoming*, and as a result *doing*, than He is about you doing things simply because of a religious idea. Rather, He longs to see you become that person who would do those things naturally. We are called human beings—not human doings—for a reason. You can do without being, but if you become, you will do automatically. God wants us to be more than we ever thought possible and hence invites us to "be holy," even as He is.

God's instruction for us to be holy is not a rejection of who we presently are. It's an invitation to make us whole and complete in every way. This idea is completely different from much of the feedback I received from my survey. Being holy is about God inviting us in to share in the essence of who He is, not about disqualifying us and driving us away.

Rather than His holiness making Him untouchable, His holiness is His invitation saying, "I want to touch you in the deepest way." One of the things that amazed people about Jesus when He walked the earth was how intimately involved He was with the people the world called degenerate. He was *accused* of being a friend of "sinners." When all of the religious muckety-mucks were in the temple commending one another on how righteous they were, Jesus, the most righteous man to walk the earth, is spending time in the homes of soon-to-be-former prostitutes and other unique types. What seemed to rouse some people even more was when Jesus not only engaged the outcasts, but would both approach and touch grossly diseased lepers, which was an unthinkable thing to do at the time. Jesus proved with His very life that holiness was something to be shared with all people, especially those who needed it the most. At the end of the day, God isn't into putting us down or making us feel less than. He wants us to be whole and complete just like Him.

The Beauty of Spiritual Intimacy

Now that you understand that holiness doesn't work against you, but instead works for you, the question is how do you become holy? The answer can be found in one word that is the path to holiness—*worship*. Worship is the key to becoming whole. But what exactly is worship? This is another word that's often misunderstood. It isn't that God is confusing or perplexing—He's just mysterious. God most definitely can be known and followed, but it's important that you first and foremost understand His heart. Many questions and confusing ideas about God are quickly cleared up when we wrap our minds around His character. There are times when I may not know exactly what God is doing, but I still have peace. This is because I've learned that even when I can't see God's hand, I can always rely on His heart. There is one thing that I will never doubt, and it's that God is always for me and will never be against me.

Worship is spiritual intimacy with God. It's not just a spiritual ritual to satisfy our religious conscience. It's a beautiful and amazing encounter with God that He desires for us to experience on a regular basis. There are so many benefits to worship, and the greatest one is that through it we change and are made whole and complete. There's nothing like it!

One widespread misconception about worship is that it can only be accomplished in a building like a church or a temple. The fact is, we can worship God *anywhere* because He is *everywhere*. He is Spirit, and we worship Him spiritually.

How do we worship, and what exactly happens when we do? Here is everything you need to know. You are about to become a lean, mean worshiping machine. Remember, you're not worshiping for the sake of worshiping. God is not into producing religious robots. God's promise is not only to complete His plans for you, but His promise is also to make you complete in the process. This is important because the epic idea that motivated your birth is carried out by a whole you. Worship is what God has ordained to make you spiritually whole. This is what shapes you for purpose and destiny.

Seven Steps to Wholeness

There are seven basic spiritual disciplines that create a transformational worship experience with God.

1. Humility

The first discipline is humility. In worship we are approaching the Almighty God, the Creator of the heavens and the earth. Acknowledging Him in this way is vital. Not because He needs you to, but because *you* need you to. Let me explain. I'm sure you've heard of the phrase *the fear of God*. This "fear" isn't about being afraid of God or nervously approaching Him. It's really not about fear at all—it's about being in awe, wonder, and deep reverence because of who you're in the midst of. God doesn't want any of us to be afraid of Him. That defeats the whole purpose of worship and what He aims for us to get out of it. It's about seeing Him right, honoring Him, and positioning yourself in His presence in a way that will allow you to receive the best He has to offer. It's not a peer-to-peer relationship. It's a Father-to-child relationship. No matter how old we get in this life, from eight to eighty—He will always see us as His child. Humility says, "God, I recognize that you are so much greater than I am. Lord, you are endless and unsearchable." It's to say, "God, I am the work of your hands—you fashioned me and formed me." We don't come to God with everything already figured out. We come to Him in reverence and humility desiring His wisdom, guidance, and help.

2. Focus

The second discipline is focus. There are so many things that compete for our attention and focus in life. God Himself has to compete with so many other things. In order to worship we have to learn to block out distracting thoughts and ideas so we can focus on the invisible God. We also must focus to get a heavenly perspective about things. God's thoughts are so much higher than our thoughts, and His perspective is so much loftier. When we worship we have to focus our mind on things higher than the realm of things that we see, feel, and touch. We have to establish our thoughts in the vast heavenly realm where God lives and where all things are possible. This elevates our mind and our perspective on the things around us. Great obstacles seem so much smaller when you have elevated your mind to see them from God's vantage point. Focusing on what's above is a key part of worship.

3. Openness

Openness is the third and perhaps the most important part of worship. In the process of worship, in order to maximize what God wants to do in your life you have to open up to Him. This may be the hardest part. To be open requires trust. Especially to the degree of openness that worship requires. In order to open up your entire being to God you have to believe in the way He feels about you. You have to be convinced that He loves you endlessly and there is nothing that can separate you from His love. You have to know that God has the ability to see every part of you—the good, the bad, and the ugly—and yet none of it affects the way He feels. God's love is unconditional. It's unique from any other type of love. It's not predicated by what you do. Your actions don't disqualify it, nor can they increase or decrease His love for you. He just loves you, simply because you're you. The areas we sometimes have the tendency to want to keep from God are the very areas His love will heal. You can be vulnerable with God because He is safe. He will never abuse, take advantage of, or condemn your transparency. You're accepted by Him already—just the way you are. God doesn't get mad at you or feel disappointed in you. He loves you forward and when He speaks to you, He is always lifting you up. He knows the plans that He has for you—plans to prosper you and not to harm you. You are His child, and you will never be a disgrace. God sees you—the real you—and loves you. Trust Him with your whole self, open up to Him and receive His love. There's nothing like it.

4. Surrender

The fourth essential in worship is surrender. Since you know the way He feels about you and that He only wants *for* you and not *from* you, you can fully surrender. Surrendering is you saying to God, "I trust you. I recognize I have my own ideas and dreams about how things should go, but while I am here in your presence I'm going to relinquish my control of my life to You. I choose to surrender my path into the hands of the one who holds the epic idea for my life."

God loves it when we trust Him enough to rely exclusively on His will for our lives. It thrills Him to see us have enough faith to be willing to surrender our own dreams and ideas for *His*. There was a time in Abraham's life when God tested him and commanded him to offer up his promised son, Isaac. I can't even imagine being placed in such a position. It was a test from the start, but Abraham didn't know it. He had so much faith that he nearly went through with it before God halted him. Abraham must have figured that if God was telling him to sacrifice his dream, He had an even greater dream in store. He trusted God's heart along with His perfect track record and chose to surrender his dream to God. What Abraham quickly discovered was that God not only gave him his dream back, but He multiplied it in ways Abraham could never have done himself. Sometimes what keeps us from the enormous dream that God has for us is our refusal to surrender our own dreams into His hands. Having the spirit of surrender and giving God an open-ended yes are significant keys in worship.

5. Receiving

The fifth step in the worship process is to receive. By this time in your worship encounter you have positioned your heart in a way that pleases God and He begins to pour into you. Wisdom, insight, and revelation will begin to flow your way. Things start to become crystal clear. This is my favorite part of worship. God will even give you knowledge of things and new ideas. I've received life-changing concepts during the receiving portion of my worship encounter. God's knowledge and insight is vast and endless. He knows everything. He is the master of witty ideas and inventions. One thought in your time of worship can radically change your life, your family's, and the lives of everyone around you. I've received ideas about business that have increased my net worth. I've received strategies on how to grow our church and make it more effective. I've gained insight and wisdom to resolve conflicts that seemed to never end. Just a few minutes in the place of worship with God can change your life and circumstances dramatically.

6. Becoming

Becoming one with God is the sixth step in the process of worship. The deepest level in worship is when your spirit becomes one with God's spirit. It's when you have opened yourself up entirely to God and have fully surrendered. This allows God's spirit to penetrate yours because there is no part of you that is resisting Him and it creates a oneness between you and God.

What closely reflects this in the physical world is the act of intimacy between a husband and wife. In one example of this type of intimacy, the wife undresses herself completely so nothing stands between her and her husband. She completely trusts her husband and shares her most intimate parts with him. She has made the decision to give him her body and soul. They become one. At that moment their minds, bodies, spirits, and souls are tied together, creating a very special bond. If you were to take away all of the sensuality and physical aspects from this process, it would mirror very closely the process of our intimacy with God during worship. He wants us to trust Him with every part of us and allow His Spirit to be intertwined with ours. This is what begins the process of making us whole.

7. Transformation

The seventh and last step in the worship process is transformation. This is the end goal and apex of worship. Once we have fixed our minds on God, have opened up to Him, and have allowed His spirit to penetrate ours, there's a divine exchange. We surrender our weaknesses for His strengths. We give up our fears in exchange for His love. He mends our brokenness and makes us whole. We start seeing things differently and start viewing life through clearer lenses. We become happier, freer, and more comfortable in our own skin. Blind spots in our lives that once caused self-destructive behavior are revealed and healed. Life becomes more exciting and optimistic than ever before. We fall in love more and more with life, ourselves, and with the God who gave it all to us. It's a progressive journey to wholeness that never stops until we, one day, see Jesus face to face.

One passage puts it this way:

But we all, with unveiled face, beholding as in a mirror the glory of the Lord, are being transformed into the same image from glory to glory, just as by the Spirit of the Lord. (2 Corinthians 3:18)

This passage is saying that we can approach God with transparency, not having to hide anything from God for fear of rejection or condemnation. To look at Him, in essence, is to look into a mirror. The mirror of God's image reflects a new image of ourselves back to us. The image that is being reflected is not the present you, but rather the *you* that was in God's mind before you were born. When you look into God's eyes through worship, His eyes reflect back to you a greater image of yourself. The more you worship, the more you see that image. The more you see that image, the more you become it. This continues over and over again as you worship, constantly transforming you into that glorious image from level to level. This is what God's spirit does to you in worship, and by doing so, is consistently making you whole. It takes a whole you to fulfill God's epic idea for your life, and worship is how you get there.

Remember, being holy is about you becoming who you were intended to be; God's creation having nothing broken, lacking, or missing. Approach God daily with humility, focus, and openness. This is worship. As you surrender to God He will pour His love into you and show you things that transcend what you could ever imagine. Your spirit will become one with His and you'll be transformed into the image God envisioned before you were born. This is the meaning of holiness—to be whole in every way.

Chapter 11

THE END OF FEAR

I often wonder how different our world would be without the existence of fear. Even with all of the advancements that people have made throughout the ages, could we be even further ahead if fear was not a factor? I've heard it said before that the wealthiest place on the planet is the graveyard. The graveyard is full of people who died with untapped potential inside because they were too afraid to live out their dreams. I'm convinced that fear is the most costly thief in all of human existence. But the person that is committed to realizing God's epic dream for their life is going to have to overcome this paralyzing foe, and we are going to discuss how to do that very thing. Fear is not something to be managed—fear is something to be ended in your life altogether.

If you are honest, you might be thinking that the idea of ending fear in your life is a little over the top. Can anybody truly rid themselves of *all* fear? Isn't it normal that we fear a little bit sometimes? Won't fear always be around? You may even be thinking that a little fear every now and again is helpful for you in some way. Let me be direct here—fear is never an asset. It's always a liability and will always subtract from your life. This is why fear can't be tolerated, and with God's help, you can have victory over it and live the epic life of purpose that God has ordained for you.

The best definition I've heard for fear is the acronym FEAR. It stands for false evidence appearing real. This is exactly what fear is. Fear paints a picture that communicates an end that is different from the future that God has promised you. It starts off as a thought, and if the thought goes uncontested it becomes an idea with its own vivid imagery, and before you know it you have been paralyzed by the perception of a reality that isn't real. This paralysis keeps you from moving forward in faith and optimism, and as a result you can miss what God intended for you in any given moment. This is why fear is dangerous. It distracts you from what God is really doing, and if you're not careful you'll begin to attract results that are the opposite of what God has for you. Remember, Peter had to overcome fear so he could walk on water, and when you overcome yours, the miraculous will happen for you too. You weren't created to fear— you were created to triumph. Here's a passage that echoes this truth perfectly:

> For God has not given us a spirit of fear, but of power and of love and of a sound mind. (2 Timothy 1:7)

So much for the question about whether or not fear is needed. We see here the answer is a resounding—absolutely not! When God created you He didn't give you a spirit of fear. On the contrary, He gave you power, love, and a sound mind. Now you may be asking how these specific three things (power, love, and a sound mind) are the opposite of fear. I'll explain by discussing them one by one. Let's begin with the word *power*.

Fear Points Power in the Wrong Direction

The average person has no concept of just how powerful he or she really is. Each of us was created in the image of God, the Creator. This means that we have an inherent power to create things. This creative ability is based upon what we think about and what we can imagine. The process of creation is this: you think it, you imagine it, you meditate on it, you envision it, you speak about it, and then you take action toward it. This is how things are created through your life and are *rooted* in your thought life. This ability can be used to create positive and constructive things as well as negative and destructive things because the creative ability itself is neutral. It's God's desire, however, that His children use it for good through receiving His good thoughts and aligning our imaginations with His epic plan for our lives.

This is why we have to be very selective with our thought life. Everyone must become thought-regulators. You have to become a gatekeeper over your own mind, because what you create is determined by what you think. When a person fears it is because a negative or untrue thought has been introduced to their mind. This is not always in your control, but you can minimize your exposure to these types of thoughts by regulating what your eyes see and what your ears hear. This will help, but you will still have to deal with an unsolicited thought or two. There is no way around the introduction of a negative thought, but what you do next is critical. You have to be diligent about quickly arresting every illegitimate thought that enters your mind and causes you to fear, because if that thought goes uncontested it *will* create something. Even if it doesn't manifest something destructive in the natural world, if will manifest something destructive in the world of your mind.

Fear is a terrorist and has every intention of robbing you of the power to produce the positive things you were created to bring forth. Fear's ultimate objective is to hold you captive in a world of false evidence appearing real, until you've been robbed of every opportunity to progress toward your purpose. The greatest threat to your potential is fear.

Another way to read Jeremiah 29:11 is like this:

*"For I know the **thoughts** that I think toward you," says the LORD, "**thoughts** of peace and not of evil, to give you a future and a hope."*

When we submit our mind to God's thoughts of prosperity and progress, we become empowered by those thoughts to create what He's declared. When a fearful idea is introduced, we have to reject it at the gate of our mind, disqualify it as invalid, and continue meditating on God's good promises for us. If we ever allowed a fearful thought to replace a God thought, we would be giving away the power we've been given to create something awesome in exchange for a thought that would otherwise subtract from us. The remedy is to be so full of God's vision for your future, and to so consistently think on the promises He's made to you, that a negative or fearful thought couldn't even stand a chance.

Fear Is an Infection of the Mind

The earlier passage also describes a sound mind as the opposite of fear. This is true, because when a person fears they are no longer able to think rationally. Fear shuts down hope and vision, causing our perspective to be restricted, limited, and gloomy. It causes a person to operate abnormally and make decisions from the place of panic and self-preservation, instead of from a place of faith and optimism. Fear is a distorter of reality. It lies to you. You start seeing things that aren't there. It makes you run when no one is pursuing. It makes you freeze when you are supposed to be running. It's your enemy in an interview. You've rehearsed what you will say in the room a thousand times, but when you get there you become disoriented and begin to trip over your own words. You think to yourself, "What just happened? I was Meryl Streep in the mirror, but at the audition I completely fell apart." I'll tell you what happened—fear happened. Fear's goal is to ruin your life and rob you of your destiny.

Fear wants to own and control you. It wants to make your decisions for you. It will cause you to settle for plan B or C by telling you to take what's in front of you or end up with nothing. It tells you that you can't do something, and therefore you never try. It intimidates you by telling you not to even speak your ideas, because if you do they will be rejected and you'll be humiliated. As a result, many people shrink and acquiesce instead of asserting themselves and succeeding because of their revolutionary vision. Fear will also threaten a future of loneliness unless you settle with a mate who, at best, is a six out of ten. Fear will place limits and boundaries on your life and hold you back from the vast possibilities your life promises. It's a nasty virus. It aims to shut down your creativity. It wants to stifle your ability to manifest the great things God has ordained for your life. Fear is the most sinister of all terrorists in the human experience and must never be tolerated.

The great news is that you don't have to entertain it. God did not give you the spirit of fear. He gave you a *different* spirit. He gave you an overcoming spirit of power, love, and soundness of mind. For every negative or fearful thought that may attempt to come to your mind, there is an even greater positive and encouraging thought to supplant it. The key is being committed to not allowing any anti-you thought to exist in your mind. You have to cease to exist to any idea that doesn't promise to prosper you and give you a future and a hope. You have to make your mind work for you and not against you. Remember, your mind isn't in control of you—you are in control of your mind. You decide what you will meditate on, and fearful thoughts are unwelcome.

The Love of God Makes Fear Irrelevant

Allow me to share a vision that changed my life forever. I was lying in bed early one morning and out of nowhere there was a profound spiritual image in front of me. I couldn't make out the face, but the eyes were very familiar. They were piercing and looked right through every part of me. In an instant, there was no longer any question in my mind about who this was. It was Jesus. There were a few things that stood out to me about the essence of the One who appeared to me. Firstly, His countenance was unique in that it could not be tied to a single people-group. He represented all of humanity, yet had no ethnic distinction. There was nothing that I could associate with a specific race or nationality. He embodied all of humanity but was fully spirit.

The second thing that stood out was the power that He possessed. I had never experienced anything like it. His very presence commanded the attention of the universe without Him saying a word or even flinching a muscle. If He simply willed that Mount Rushmore would become a negligible mound of dust, it would effortlessly become so. He emitted so much strength that if He were to stand at the edge of the sea and desire that the ocean stand straight up, becoming miles high, exposing its depths and foundations, it would just happen without Him having to let out even the faintest sound. I'd never seen power like that before. This was the greatest power I could ever imagine, yet it was fully restrained.

The third thing that I noticed about Him was the intense, piercing gaze in His eyes. He was totally consumed with *something*. Something had His complete attention in a way that He could not be distracted from. I wondered momentarily what great thing was commanding His attention in such a way, before it dawned on me what He was looking at. He was staring at me. Then I realized that it wasn't just me, but it was about every human being who had ever entered this world. He was absolutely consumed with us. This was the true God. This was not a God of hate, but the One true God of absolute love who was totally obsessed with the creation He personally fashioned and formed Himself.

The last thing that stood out to me during this life-altering encounter was the atmosphere in which this encounter was happening. This was the first time I had experienced the pure love of God. It was not an emotion—it was a realm. God's love was so strong and penetrating that it created an atmosphere around me that was so transformational, it would instantaneously and completely disarm anyone who had unforgiveness, offense, or bitterness toward another in their heart. There was an incredible healing presence in this atmosphere of God's love. Anger would immediately dissipate and fear was nonexistent. What God was exposing to me was His raw love, and it was rapturous. My friend, if you only knew the way that God loves you and how *into you* He truly is, you would never fear another day in your life.

Here is a great passage that describes the power of God's love to end fear in our lives forever:

> *And we have known and believed the love that God has for us. God is love, and he who abides in love abides in God, and God in him. Love has been perfected among us in this: that we may have boldness in the day of judgment; because as He is, so are we in this world. There is no fear in love; but perfect love casts out fear, because fear involves torment. But he who fears has not been made perfect in love. We love Him because He first loved us. (1 John 4:16–19)*

There are a few things plainly stated in this passage I'd like us to look at.

The first thing it says is that God is love. This means that the very essence of God *is* love. It's a unique type of love. It's not a brotherly love or a romantic love. It's a distinct love that only comes from Him. It's an unconditional love. It's pure and will never change. It's hard to envision because it is unlike any other type of love we have ever experienced in life. Even those of us who understand this and strive to channel God's love to others will still fall short because of the fallibility of our own channel. But God's love is direct, pure, and profound. There's nothing like it.

The passage goes on to speak of the effect that God's love has on those who understand it. It speaks of them being bold and confident, even when they have to be judged by God. This is a major statement. We are talking about being in a place of having to give an account of the entirety of our lives before the Almighty God, yet because of His love we are able to do so with boldness and confidence. Knowing that you are loved in this way doesn't produce self-righteous arrogance. That's not what I'm talking about. In fact, this love has nothing to do with what a person has done or didn't do. This confidence is not about someone's lifestyle, but is attributed to that person's revelation of how much God loves them. If God's love will free you from fear at the most important hearing of your life, surely it will free you from the fear of any threat you'll face in life.

The passage goes on to say that there is no fear in love. Since we also know that God is love, this passage is ultimately saying that fear is nonexistent in God. The passage, in fact, says that perfect love casts out fear because fear torments people. God's plan is to prosper you and not to harm you. Anything that brings you pain and suffering in life, God is ultimately against. This doesn't mean that in life you will never suffer. It just means that God has made provision in His ultimate plan for your life to bring relief, healing, and total restoration for any suffering that your life may bring. The passage concludes with a powerful truth that you must understand. It states that the individual who fears has in that moment lost sight of the revelation of God's love or has never been introduced to it. The passage reads *he who fears has not been made perfect in love*. That word that was translated *perfect* comes from a Greek word that means, once again, "complete." What is being relayed here is that God's love is designed to make you whole. The revelation of the love of God is what heals you from all fear. The passage is saying that if you fear, the reason is simple. You just haven't matured in your understanding of God's love yet. Don't see fear as a roadblock. See it as an opportunity to grow in the liberating knowledge of God's love. He longs to show it to you. Soon you will say what the writer of this passage says—"I love Him because He first loved me."

The Characteristics of God's Love

I could write an entire book on the characteristics of God's love but wanted to highlight a few of them here for you to consider. It's not just *knowing* that God loves you that puts an end to fear—it's knowing *how* He loves you and what you can expect as a result of it. Here are just a few things:

- **God's love gives.** Expect to see God open heaven over you from time to time and awe you with love notes and gifts that have His fingerprints all over them.
- **God's love corrects.** Don't mistake God's love through correction for Him being upset with you. God wants the best for you, and your journey to purpose is His best. If He sees you veering off course He will initiate a *course correction.* They aren't always fun, but trust me—you will thank Him in the end.
- **God's love protects.** Expect God's love to protect you from dangers that are seen and those that are unseen. He's watching over you right now and protecting your life.
- **God's love redeems.** God's forgiveness and mercy are abundant. He longs to redeem the lives and reputations of His loved ones. No matter how far you may have gotten away from God, part of His very nature is redemption. He doesn't even remember our mistakes, so there's no need for you to either. Embrace redemption today. Your best days are ahead.
- **God's love restores.** Sometimes in life you lose things. If you read about Job you can learn a whole lot about that. However, losing isn't the end of the story. Anything God allows you to lose in life, He will cause to be restored at the proper time. Your life may have been filled with burned-down businesses, relationships, and more. But God is a master at causing beauty to rise from the ashes of life. Stay hopeful; your restoration is near.
- **God's love is never-ending.** Nothing can ever separate you from God's love. Even if you tried to reject it, it would still be

there. God's love pursues you. Nothing will ever change that. David once wrote a song about the faithfulness of God's love. David writes, "Surely goodness and mercy shall follow me all the days of my life" (see Ps. 23:6). Goodness and mercy are attributes of God's love, and they will be with you forever.

The end of fear can be a reality in your life. You may not be able to keep a fearful thought from coming, but you can surely prevent it from staying. Remember, any thought that makes you afraid is a futile argument against God's love. You only need to remind yourself of how God feels about you and meditate on His promises. Never let a fearful thought attempt to eclipse your optimistic view of your future. Remember, God isn't finished with you. He's just getting started. As you grow in the knowledge of God's love, fear is going to pack its bags and leave. God's love is going to give you a new reason to live. Without fear, your entire universe will be re-colored— brighter, and full of light, love, and hope. God's love is going to evict fear and increase your faith. As you grow in your intimacy with God, He is going to make your journey to purpose more thrilling and liberating than you could have ever imagined.

Chapter 12

THE UNIVERSAL PURPOSE

One thing I've learned through being awakened to purpose is that destiny is more than a destination—it's the journey itself. The things that transpire on your way to fulfilling purpose are just as significant as the purpose itself. God's idea of purpose is more than fulfilling your unique and distinct assignments. There is another aspect to purpose—a *universal* purpose that each of us have, that's a key part of God's ultimate plan. This universal purpose is God's highest intention for you and is more important than anything you'll ever accomplish. The universal purpose is rooted in God's idea of who you truly are, and is about you progressively becoming God's interpretation of you through encounters that occur on your path to purpose. In other words, the best part about your purpose is the *becoming* that takes place on your journey to it.

Everything on the path to purpose means something. There is nothing that happens in your life that shouldn't have. Your successes, failures, mistakes, hurts, and joys are all playing a part in developing you for God's epic plan. Have you ever found yourself in certain situations that make you look up and say, "Okay, God—what is this about?" Well the truth is, everything is always about something. Who we truly are is so beyond where we currently are. It requires a variety of things to shape us into the image of greatness God knew before we were born. Purpose requires us to change and grow. As our life and character matures, purpose happens. The unfolding of God's plan happens concurrently with the unfolding of us. The reason why the fulfillment of our purpose doesn't happen overnight is because our growth, change, and transformation take time.

Scripture says:

> *And do not be conformed to this world, but be transformed by the renewing of your mind, that you may prove what is that good and acceptable and perfect will of God. (Romans 12:2)*

You know what I'm going to say about this Scripture, right? You guessed it—"This is one of my favorite passages of Scripture." As you get to know me, you'll realize that I have a lot of favorite passages. In fact, the whole thing is good when you understand the heart behind the One who inspired it. It's certainly challenging at times, but it's always good. It stretches you beyond your perceived limits and elevates you to the reality of your potential. Thank God for anything in your life that does that. With that being said, thank you for accommodating my digression—now back to the subject at hand.

In this passage the first thing that is mentioned is a warning for us to not become conformers. The reason we shouldn't conform is because each of us is a unique idea in God's mind with a specific identity, purpose, and calling. If we are born into this realm and conform to what already is, then what becomes of God's epic idea for us? To take things further, God's plan for us is to impact the world we are born into—not to conform to it. So from the get-go, the passage instructs you to proactively embrace your distinction.

As the passage continues, the contrast is made between conforming and being transformed. It's the difference between regression and progression. When you conform to what is, it's a regression away from what God originally intended. When you are transformed, it's your progression toward the epic idea that motivated your birth. The passage reads:

But be transformed by the renewing of your mind, that you may prove what is that good and acceptable and perfect will of God.

God's epic idea concerning you is described perfectly in this passage. The more accurate translation of the last phrase in the passage would better read like this:

That you may be so clear in God's purpose for your life that you'll be able to test and therefore prove that your life is in alignment with the plan that God calls beneficial, the one He is in full agreement with, and that which is His perfect and complete intention for your life.

Wow! Who wouldn't want to live this kind of life and have the fulfillment that comes with this much assurance? The truth is, this is exactly what God intends for all of us. He doesn't want His children shooting in the dark. He wants you to live a focused life, hitting the mark at every turn and experiencing the excitement and blessing of partnering with the founder of the Universe. He longs to reveal to you the reason why you are here and to expose you to a life that is nothing short of epic.

Your Destination Is Transformation

The word in this passage that was translated *transformed* is the Greek word *metamorphoo*. It's where we get our English word *metamorphosis*, and it describes a very specific type of change. It's the kind of change that moves in one progressive direction and is never reversed. It's a permanent change. This word is used to describe the process that a caterpillar undergoes when it is turning into a butterfly. The process of the caterpillar becoming a butterfly is a brilliant illustration of the spiritual transformation that God intends for your life.

What's eye-opening about this process is that God's highest intention for the caterpillar was never for it to remain a caterpillar—it was always to become a butterfly. The caterpillar and later its cocoon are just parts of the process to develop what God had ultimately envisioned from the start. We know this because even while a caterpillar is still developing inside its egg, it already begins to grow something that science calls imaginal discs. The imaginal discs are what will later become the wings, legs, and eyes of the butterfly after the transformation process. In other words, before the caterpillar is even born, God has already made provision for what it will be in the future. The same thing is true with you. Remember, everything in the natural mirrors a spiritual reality. Before you were even placed in your mother's womb God knew exactly what He intended for you to be. No matter what your life may look like now, what God has ultimately envisioned is nothing short of breathtaking. Your destiny is truly epic, but you'll have to go through a transformation process to get there.

Another interesting fact about the process of the caterpillar becoming a butterfly is the caterpillar's involvement in its own transformation. At a certain point in the caterpillar's life a shift takes place. It stops feeding itself and hangs upside down on a twig and spins itself into a cocoon. While inside the cocoon a radical transformation takes place, and when it's complete a beautiful butterfly emerges. It becomes a brand-new creation with flying ability, enabling it to experience life at a higher dimension as God had intended from the very start.

But what happens to the caterpillar that was inside the cocoon? Quite frankly, it dies. During the transformation process the caterpillar digests itself by releasing enzymes that dissolve all of its tissues and becomes mush. If you were to cut the cocoon open at the right time, caterpillar soup would ooze out. At this stage the only parts of the caterpillar that remain are those imaginal discs that will become the eyes, wings, and legs of the new creation. This process closely resembles what you and I will have to undergo in our own spiritual metamorphosis. In order to experience the transformation that leads to the fulfilling of God's dream for your life, like the caterpillar you'll have to submit to the process that leads to the emergence of a brand-new you; even if it means dying to the old you.

Transformation is not automatic. It requires a decision and action. What if the caterpillar never stopped eating caterpillar food and refused to subject itself to the process of change that led to its glorious new life? That answer is simple. It would have lived and died a caterpillar, missing the unfathomable opportunity to become a butterfly. Just as the caterpillar had these imaginal discs that later activated its potential to fly, we too have the ability to become more than we could ever imagine. The way we keep our greatness out of the graveyard of potential is by submitting ourselves to the process of transformation that God has orchestrated for our lives.

The Beginning of Transformation

You may be thinking, "I get the scientific process of a caterpillar's transformation to a butterfly, but what does my transformation look like in practical terms? How does this work for me?"

The process of spiritual transformation has many parts and spans various dimensions, but it always starts with the same thing—a person being exposed to the greatest story ever told.

When I was nine years old my mother was inspired to take me to a church service. She was not a religious woman, nor did she attend church for herself, but she thought it would be a wise decision as a single parent raising an African American boy in one of the toughest neighborhoods in the United States. I remember sitting in the pews with my mom and hearing the preacher talk about Jesus. The church was almost entirely black and it had a choir that swayed, a pipe organ, a whole lot of shouting, and fiery preaching. To be honest, I didn't really understand anything that was happening. It was very strange, but everyone else seemed to enjoy it. I did, however, keep feeling drawn to this Jesus person that the preacher was describing.

Then one day, after the sermon the pastor invited anyone from the congregation to come forward if they wanted to embrace Jesus and receive Him into their life. My mom tells the story best, describing how I turned to her with a look in my eyes that said, "Mom, we should go up there." Apparently she couldn't resist my baby browns, so she let out a sigh, clasped my hand, and we made our way down what felt like the longest aisle in the world. We ended up in front of the church standing at the altar. I remember the pastor leading us in a simple prayer to receive Jesus into our hearts. That day I knew something special happened deep inside of me. A profound spiritual deposit was made in my heart that God would later draw from to manifest my full transformation.

What happened next in my life isn't what you'd imagine following such a dramatic spiritual encounter. You would think that the story would continue with me becoming a faithful church member, singing in the children's choir, attending Sunday school, and becoming a good little Christian boy. Well, not so much. As a matter of fact the exact opposite happened. I stopped going to church regularly because it bored me to death. I did sing in the choir, but it was only when my mom forced me to. In grade school I was usually the brightest in my class, but I chose the role of class clown and regularly entertained my way right into the principal's office. So much for the good little Christian boy.

I was, however, a great kid with a pure heart and had my own personal relationship with God. His spirit would often convict me when I did something I knew was wrong. The only thing was, I couldn't seem to overcome the part of me that was naturally inclined to push the limits and go astray. What I didn't understand then was that receiving Jesus and welcoming His spirit into my life wasn't the end of transformation—it was just the beginning. What I would learn years later was that the fullness of transformation happens through continuously having your mind renewed. It's like the caterpillar. Making the decision to stop eating what it had grown accustomed to was just the beginning of its metamorphosis. It then had to subject itself to a predetermined process that involved various stages of change and growth. When that process was complete, it would become the glorious creation God intended it to be.

Doing Away with the Old Mind

When I made the decision as a little boy to receive Jesus into my heart, what I didn't know was that I was only receiving the seed of my transformation. What I got that day was the Spirit of God, who would become the facilitator of my metamorphosis. This Spirit would be with me my entire life to guide, direct, and to teach me along my way. The Spirit would be my personal purpose guide long before I had a clue that my life even had a specific purpose. This is such a fascinating aspect of God. He knows our ending from the beginning and has His hand on our lives guiding us toward purpose while we are in complete oblivion. He is so patient with us, but then again, why wouldn't He be, knowing the outcome of our lives from the onset?

I later learned that the Spirit I had received was called the Holy Spirit. It's the spirit of God Himself. The Holy Spirit embodies God's thoughts, His wholeness, and of course contains all of His epic ideas for each of His children. This means, I actually had access to the revelation of my purpose and the roadmap to get there from the time of my encounter with God as a child.

Many times in life our challenge isn't that we don't have access to what we need or lack the ability to accomplish something. It's just that too often we aren't aware of what we *do* have. It's true that receiving the Holy Spirit is just the first step to transformation, but what you receive gives you everything you need to fulfill all of the subsequent steps. The process from there is to continue to renew your mind with the knowledge that the Spirit freely gives. It's through the renewing of your mind that you are transformed in a way that causes you to *become* and to accomplish what God has envisioned for your life.

Let's look at the passage again:

And do not be conformed to this world, but be transformed by the renewing of your mind, that you may prove what is that good and acceptable and perfect will of God.

There's something that is implied in the text that we cannot afford to overlook. It has to do with what is being indirectly said about the current condition of our mind. If we are being told in the passage that in order to be transformed for our purpose and destiny we must renew our mind, that tells us there is something lacking in the mind that we presently possess.

Let's revisit the caterpillar's transformation to better understand this point. First, it had to go through a process of dying in its former state. There was nothing it could take of its old identity into its new one. The only exception was the imaginal discs, which were given to ensure it became the butterfly it was destined to be. As the former creature was being dissolved, a renewal was taking place, and the new creation emerged. The caterpillar's identity, though once sufficient, now became a barrier to where its future was taking it. To bring its same essence and characteristics into its new life would not work. It would still try to crawl when it should now be flying. The caterpillar that it used to be had to decrease, so the butterfly it was destined to be could come forth. This process of renewal continues until the full transformation takes place.

It works the same way with us. Before our minds get renewed, they were shaped by many things we were exposed to in life. Although good exists here, there is much that is broken and harmful and we can't help but be exposed to these limiting environments. There is sickness, disease, hatred, and murder. Our world has pain, insecurity, crime, and betrayal. There's molestation, abuse, addiction, and suicide. The list goes on and on, and we can't afford to forget the fact that at the end of all, there's death itself. These things are not a part of God's epic plan for us. As a matter of fact, the very existence of these things in our world cause trauma to the human spirit and psyche. Our innocence was stripped away from birth by what we experienced, witnessed, or simply heard about. We've even adapted and learned how to function in a world where traumatic things happen every day. This is a great testament to the power of the human will, but is this really what God intended? We've become so desensitized to it that we even recreate that same trauma in our entertainment, which you'd think would be the place we'd turn to escape it. We perpetuate life's tragedies in video games and allow our young people to rehearse death repetitively. All of these things have had an effect on our minds, but usually it happens subconsciously.

Even our hope has fallen victim to this mind-set. The idea of crime being eliminated is unthinkable, so we build more jails and hire more police. We are convinced that our teenagers will never stop the dangerous practice of having sex too soon, so we hand out condoms at school. We are trapped in a world full of limitation and restriction—far from the wholeness and liberty that God's plan promises.

These are the types of realities that cause many to question the very existence of God. *If there is a God, then how could He allow such trauma, brokenness, and pain to take place in the lives of His children? Where is God? What is He doing about all of this?* These are legitimate questions I would never pretend to have all the answers to, but what I do know is this. It all comes down to the question of who is Jesus and what did He do?

There is no figure in human history more debated among people than Jesus. There is no one throughout the ages who has drawn more controversy from people, both of faith and those who have no faith, than Him. Most major religions of the world acknowledge Him but tell completely different stories about Him. Jesus' life was known to involve miracles, but it seems the greatest miracle is that no matter how many people feel compelled to define Him, all seem to come to different conclusions. This isn't the case for anyone else in life—with the exception of God Himself. No normal life could have that type of impact on the entire world, so the question is, Who is Jesus—really?

There is one passage that I believe plainly answers that question and also gives insight into what God is doing as a response to the things that are happening in our world.

> *For He made Him who knew no sin to be sin for us, that we might become the righteousness of God in Him. (2 Corinthians 5:21)*

Okay. I am going to restate this passage in the context of purpose and then explain what it all means. This passage tells us that:

> *God—the Creator of all things—made Him (Jesus), who Himself (Jesus) had no sin, to become the sin of this world, so that we all could realize our universal purpose, which is to become Godlike in Him (Jesus).*

There are a few primary ideas in this passage that we need to look at. The first idea is sin, the second is Jesus, and the third is our destiny. Let's start with understanding sin.

There's a Greek word that is translated *sin* in the Scripture. It's the word *harmartema*.

This word that was translated *sin* doesn't mean what many people think. Sin doesn't mean wicked, bad, or evil. It means "to fall short." The literal translation means "to miss the mark." If this is a fact, then the million-dollar question is, what are we falling short of? What mark are we missing? Here's your answer. The mark that sin causes us to miss is the fulfillment of God's epic idea for our lives. Remember—the caterpillar wasn't God's epic idea, the butterfly was. The caterpillar, although relevant for a season, ultimately fell short of the butterfly God ultimately envisioned. In order for the butterfly to realize God's ultimate goal, the caterpillar had to be destroyed. It's the same with us. Sin, the condition that causes us to miss the mark, is the only thing that holds us back from the full unfolding of God's plan for us. Therefore, it had to be destroyed.

All of the things that are in our world—sickness, pain, betrayal, insecurity, and right up to death itself—fall way short of what God had in mind when He created us. These things are the consequence of sin, and God has made provision for the destruction of what destroys the ones He loves.

This is where Jesus comes in. Even Jesus had a purpose. He had a five-part assignment that would fulfill God's plan to finish what He started when He created man in His own image. Here is what His assignment entailed:

1. To become the entirety of the sin of the world.
2. To put sin to death in His own body.
3. To demonstrate His triumph over sin by being raised from death which is the most powerful state of sin.
4. To reproduce the same victorious phenomenon in the lives of every person who will allow it.
5. To return to earth at the appointed time for the fulfillment of sin's eradication.

For God made Jesus who had no sin to become sin for us, that we might become the righteousness of God in Jesus.

The last part of this passage is about the fulfilling of our universal purpose. Our universal purpose is to be made whole. It's to be like God. It's to be free from brokenness, insecurity, fear, and pain. Jesus set us on the path to unlocking the butterfly we all have within. Jesus coming into your life is a vital part of God's epic idea for you. This is why God makes receiving Him easy enough for a nine-year-old child to understand. All I had to do was respond to His gentle knocking on the door of my heart. When I said yes and opened the door, He came in and has been with me ever since. I've found Him to be the perfect father, teacher, counselor, and life-guide. Embracing Him was a decision far greater than any I had ever made. Without question, it is the reason for all of the success and the significance I experience in life.

Renewing Your Mind

The last part of the transformation process that leads to your wholeness is the renewing of your mind.

And do not be conformed to this world, but be transformed by the renewing of your mind, that you may prove what is that good and acceptable and perfect will of God.

You may be wondering why you have to renew your mind if you have opened up to Jesus and have received the Holy Spirit who thinks God's thoughts? Great question—here's the answer. Our mind is the last one to get God's memos. Our spirit understands, but our mind has to catch up. Remember our mind has been shaped in the context of sin for our entire life. It has to be renewed. This includes learning, unlearning, and reprocessing. What we think determines our reality. It doesn't determine actual reality, just the reality in our head. This is very important because as we think, so we are. You can never be more than what you think you are.

Many people are still blinded and enslaved by the effects of sin because they don't yet know Jesus or understand what He did. It boils down to a knowledge problem. Then you have another group of people who do know of Jesus but haven't fully grasped all that He accomplished when He came. These are only slightly better off than those who don't know Him. Then there are yet others who know Him, who understand what He did, but don't renew their mind daily. This results in them living a fair life, but still falling short of the wholeness that constant mind renewal will afford them. The caterpillar could not become every detail of the butterfly, until all that was left of the old caterpillar was gone. We can only become whole in every way when every part of the old mind is replaced with new ways of thinking, which lead to new levels of being.

The universal purpose of becoming whole creates the health and clarity needed for the awakening to your specific purpose in life. As you renew your mind with God's words, you'll move closer and closer to becoming the epic idea that God foresaw.

Part V

PURPOSE AWAKENING

Chapter 13

THE MOMENT OF CLARITY

There's something fascinating you should know about purpose. It's not something you just look up and find one day. The discovery of purpose is actually your awakening to what has always been. There's a transforming moment on the road to destiny when you realize that what you've been searching for has been with you all along. It's a time like no other on your journey to purpose. It's that moment of clarity, when your past, present, and future all sync together in one instant. In a flash, you realize everything in your life up to this point was to prepare you for the very moment you're standing in. Even things you once questioned or lamented over, instantaneously become vital pieces to the puzzle of God's plan for your life. It's the moment when everything fits in perfect alignment with your destiny and the trajectory of your life is changed forever.

My purpose awakening happened while on a family trip to Northern California. While visiting the San Francisco area I felt compelled to take my wife and children over to Oakland to visit some of the places I remembered from my early childhood. As we drove from one location to another I suddenly became overwhelmed with emotion. I was having a major epiphany. I started to realize that God had His hand on me ever since I was a child. It all began to make sense. There was a reason I was born in Oakland. There was a reason God chose the parents He did to bring me forth. There was even a reason why my parents didn't stay together. I then realized that nothing about my life had been random or arbitrary. I could see it all so clearly, and every bit of it made sense. I couldn't see it while I was in it, and there were some things I wished I could have changed, but in my awakening I discovered that everything was exactly the way it was supposed to be. All of it had shaped me into the person I had become, and without this becoming I would not have been fit for the mandate assigned to my life.

I thought about the neighborhood that I was raised in while living in Oakland. It was very ethnically diverse. I remember having friends from several ethnic backgrounds and many who were of mixed race. Diversity seemed and felt very normal to me. Once we moved to the inner city of Los Angeles, however, things were much different. I lived in an almost exclusively African American neighborhood. There was no diversity and very few interactions with people who didn't look like me. In hindsight, I realized that had I not been exposed to multiculturalism at an early age, it would have been difficult for me to integrate organically into environments of diversity. This would later become a significant key to my purpose as the church that I presently lead draws people from every nation together each week for worship. God knows exactly what He is doing and knew the exact place for me to be born so I'd be exposed to what I needed to fulfill His plan for my life.

Considering this opened me up to another understanding about purpose. In a sense, we are all born directly into ours. Here's what I mean. There's purpose in the things in our lives that shape us *for* our purpose. Where you were born has significance. Your ethnicity means something. The parents God chose for you were not a mistake. Even the parent you may have never known was part of God's design in shaping you for great things. God uses everything—the good, the bad, and the ugly—to create beauty in this world through our lives. Here's a great passage that expresses this:

And we know that all things work together for good to those who love God, to those who are the called according to His purpose. (Romans 8:28)

In that moment I understood there was synergy between everything in my past and who I had come to be. There was nothing to regret about yesterday. All of my experiences, both good and bad, immediately became counterparts working together toward the vision of God's purpose for my life. It was an indescribable time, filled with immense gratitude and freedom like never before. All fear and trepidation about the future disappeared, causing me to be full of assurance with great optimism about the destiny I had in store.

Your Purpose Finds You

There is a strategy to the timing of your purpose awakening. It can't happen too soon in your life, nor can it happen too late. There are certain things that must be in place in order for this moment to have the impact on your life it's supposed to. God doesn't awaken you to your purpose simply for knowledge's sake. This awakening is designed to create something within that becomes the *self-substance* that guarantees the completion of your life's race.

The first thing that must be in place is a certain measure of wholeness in your life. Although we're always on the journey to absolute wholeness, there are certain plateaus of healing we must reach prior to our awakening. When we begin our journey to wholeness, we all start with things in our lives that have the potential to restrict our progress. I call these things "key constraints." They are unhealthy ways of thinking that govern our approach to life and how we live it out. If these paradigms aren't healed by the renewing of our mind, they'll create blind spots that keep us from moving forward in certain areas. Have you ever seen someone go through the same situation over and over again, never seeming to get to the other side? If so, it is quite probable that the culprit in the equation is a key constraint. It could be the result of harboring unforgiveness or struggling to overcome the fear of rejection. A key constraint can play itself out in the form of an addiction or cause you to sabotage every relationship you enter into. These are the types of things God targets immediately, because without overcoming them you won't be positioned for your moment of clarity.

This awakening also can't happen until you have stepped outside of the familiar. One of the main reasons for leaving the familiar is to come out of old mind-sets. Many times our purpose is hidden right in front of us in plain sight, but our key constraints keep us from seeing it. What we see at any given moment is dependent upon the *settings* of our mind. A great analogy of this is the difference between a vulture and a hummingbird. The two birds can fly over an identical landscape but see two completely different things. The hummingbird will see a beautiful flower and be drawn to discover its scent and flavor. The vulture, on the other hand, will look right past the flower and set its sights on the dead carcass lying next to it. One bird's mind is set to see beauty, the other death. When we overcome our key constraints it gives us the hummingbird perspective and awakens us to the beauty that's already around us. As we overcome continuously, we naturally gravitate toward the purpose of our lives and will find ourselves in a moment of clarity that confirms we're in the right place at the right time. You don't find purpose, purpose finds you—at the right time. It's a timing thing, and your healing is a big part of it.

Awakening to Purpose

When thinking about my own journey to purpose, one thing that never ceases to amaze me is how much wisdom God used while guiding me to it. I have to admit, there were times when it didn't feel like wisdom when it was happening, but when the dust settled it was wisdom without a doubt.

God hid my purpose from me in plain sight for years before finally revealing it to me. In hindsight, I realize that there was enormous wisdom in Him doing so. For me to know prematurely, as a young ambitious pastor, that my purpose would involve having great influence with powerful people in Hollywood would have undoubtedly sabotaged my destiny. There was no way I could have handled that information early on. There were key constraints I needed to overcome in order to fulfill my calling successfully. Even to know that there was such a calling on my life too soon would have been a stumbling block. Destructive pride could have set in because of the promise of power. Perhaps fear of that much responsibility would have driven me away. There were still insecurities inside that lay dormant, needing to be addressed. It's possible to have an insecurity that goes undetected until you are placed in an environment that forces it to surface. It's one thing to boast about what you would never do when you are never given the opportunity to do it, but you having the opportunity to do it creates a completely different reality. Some people are quick to judge celebrities and other powerful people for their actions. What they don't realize is that if they themselves had access to the same things, they too could fall—perhaps even sooner. God's wisdom in not giving me all the facts up front was based on what He knew I could handle, and when. Before He could bring me into this pivotal moment he had to make sure that my character could sustain my calling.

The Acceleration of Purpose

When God brings you into your purpose awakening it brings your life into its proper context. Gone are the days of ambiguity and aimlessness. You now understand and are convinced about the reason for your existence. This moment of clarity lights a fire in your heart, adds a strong wind of faith to your sails, and thrusts you optimistically forward into your future. Awesome things begin to happen for you. It's like the entire universe all of a sudden recognizes you and starts working with you to fulfill your purpose. Remember the passage "all of creation eagerly awaits the revealing of the children of God"? It's as if creation itself celebrates your arrival as you finally come into full alignment with what God foreknew about you. Doors you knocked on for years all of a sudden swing open to you. It's an amazing time. This season of your life brings great acceleration. It puts you on the fast track of purpose. You'll supernaturally accomplish in one year what may have taken you five or ten years in the past. Your former wisdom is infused with a fresh understanding that you start using to live out your purpose. You finally get past a certain learning curve and are able to utilize and benefit from what your years have taught you.

Your destiny begins to come into focus. It's like you were once a ship lost at sea. Then one day you see land in the distance and begin to steer toward it. The closer you get to shore, the more precise your movements are. At first, all you could see was a big strip of land, but as you approach you're able to make out where the dock is. Before you know it, what was hardly visible in the distance becomes the very place you're standing. This is what happens in the moment of clarity. You can see clearly now and know where you are going. It causes you to manage your time better, because you can qualify or disqualify every activity based on whether or not it fits your purpose. What you do and who you do it with is no longer casually decided but carefully considered. Your purpose *is* your life. It's who you were born to be and what you were created to do. Because the vision has been made plain to you, your life becomes the most disciplined it's ever been. You start hitting the mark every time, and God can now do so much more through your life.

The Restoration of Lost Things

There is something else that takes place in the purpose awakening season. Restoration happens. Scripture is filled with promises of restoration when God's people come into alignment with Him. As a matter of fact, the ability to restore things is one of the unique characteristics of God. Many of the miracles that Jesus performed were restorative. From restoring sight to the blind to healing people with all types of debilitating disease to even restoring a man's ear that had been severed. And let's not forget about one of the greatest accounts of restoration—Jesus resurrecting the life of the dead man Lazarus. There are countless stories of God's restoration. Once while at a wedding, the guests began to panic when all the wine ran out too soon. Well guess who was invited to the party? That's right—Mr. Restoration. Jesus becomes the life of the party by turning water into wine. What's even more awesome about this story of restoration is that those who drank that new wine said that it was even better than what they had before. This gives us a very encouraging insight about God's restoration. When He restores He doesn't just put things back the way they were—He makes them even greater. There is a passage that reads:

> *Then what you had in the past will seem small compared with the great prosperity you'll have in the future. (Job 8:7 GW)*

There will be times in your life when you'll feel like you've lost something. It could be the loss of time or a sense of missed opportunities. Maybe you worked hard at something in the past and it seemed to profit little, if any at all. Perhaps you started a business or some type of organization that fell apart. You may have even felt loss because of a relationship that didn't work out. There are countless ways we experience the feeling of loss in life and it is never fun or easy. One thing to remember in those tough moments, however, is that there is no such thing as loss in purpose—only gain. The appearance of progress can be deceiving. Sometimes in order to build something grand, it will require the tearing down of something else. Always remember that God is a Creator. He has the ability to create something out of what looks like nothing. There is a verse in Isaiah that says He gives beauty for ashes (see Isa. 61:3). This is amazing! Think about it. Ashes represent what once was. When something burns to the ground all that is left is ashes, yet God says, "I'll create beauty from it." Allow God's ability to create and *re-create* to inspire you daily, especially when you're burdened with a sense of loss. All things are possible with Him, and your restoration can show up at any moment. In fact, many times what we think is lost is actually being reserved for us in God's plan waiting for the right time to be restored. Remember, God is always up to something, and it's always bigger than what we think.

I remember executive producing a music project for our church. I was able to put together an awesome team of songwriters, producers, and singers. Over the course of two years we spent a lot of time and money to create this project. Finally it was complete and we were very pleased with what we had done. We got all of our branding and packaging together, had a great musical debut, and released the project to the world. There was only one problem—the world didn't buy it. Sales for the music trickled in little by little, not seeming to have anywhere near the impact we had hoped for. Before long, we had stopped pushing the project and began to make plans for the next one. Nearly one full year of inactivity with the project had passed when I received a random phone call from the producers of a worldwide television station. They were calling to see if I would come on their show for an interview. I graciously accepted their invitation and asked them if I could present my music on the show. They heard the music, loved it, and agreed to bring my team on the show. This was God's restoration. Just when I thought that the project was dead, God stepped in and said, "It's not over until I say it's over."

When it was all said and done over half a billion households were exposed to our music and responded quite favorably. What I learned with that experience is that timing is everything. I originally thought that our investment of time and resources wasn't going to pay off. Much to my surprise, God had already calculated in our success. He took things beyond what I could have ever imagined. His plan of restoration was in full effect, He was just waiting for the right opportunity for maximum impact. In one day God made up for what I had been counting as loss over many months. God's restoration is more than just making things right. It retroactively restores what was lost during the downtime. In other words, restoration is you receiving in one day not only what was meant for that day, but for all the days that passed by and the times you felt you missed out on something. Restoration is God's specialty, and when you awaken to your purpose, the floodgates of restoration open up to you.

I don't think there's a happier time in life than the initial season of your purpose awakening. It's like being born again. God proves to you during this time that He is legit and will bring to fruition everything He's promised. It motivates you and gives you confidence about things to come. You have a clear goal now that you can safely invest your future into. You know it will work because purpose can't fail. Now it's time to move forward and witness the unfolding of God's marvelous plan for your life.

Chapter 14

THE EVOLUTION OF PURPOSE

Everything in life evolves. People evolve, societies evolve, successful organizations evolve, and even relationships evolve. Evolution is about the progressive unfolding of a thing. It's a constant reminder to us that in life we'll always be playing catch-up to what God already knows and what He's already done. When God creates something, He does so from a place that transcends time and space. Remember, God didn't start with time and space. Time and space got their start from God. Everything that God creates into the realm of time was already completed in the realm that transcends time. In other words, what becomes manifest in time is just a reflection of what's already completed in the eternal realm, outside of time. Evolution happens when the time-and-space realm catches up to what the eternal realm has *already* experienced. For this reason everything in time will constantly evolve until it finally becomes identical with the eternal.

Your purpose also goes through the process of evolution. Remember, it's the epic idea God had for you before you were born. God says, "Before I formed you in your mother's womb I knew you." God does not say *I will* know you. Instead, He uses the past tense when describing you. That's because He is talking to *the* you in time, about the reality of a completed you that transcends time. This lets us know that our lives have already been carried out and perfected in the eternal realm. Certainly, we have to walk it out, but what's being lived out has actually already been accomplished. Likewise, purpose isn't something that is revealed to you once and you're set for life. Your purpose must continue to evolve with your life, until your life is an exact resemblance of what God foreknew about you.

There is something you have to wrap your mind around when it comes to purpose. Your purpose is not an activity, destination, or location—**your purpose is an awareness**. It's the consciousness that says, "I'm here for a reason, and I'm fully committed to carrying it out." The awareness of purpose understands that no matter where you are in life you have to keep going and pursuing God's will for *every season*. The awareness of purpose says, "I haven't arrived yet and must remain open to the next instruction on purpose's path, until every detail of God's plan for me has been accomplished."

One purpose seeker in Scripture named Paul puts it this way:

Not that I have already attained, or am already perfected; but I press on, that I may lay hold of that for which Christ Jesus has also laid hold of me. (Philippians 3:12)

This is a profound insight into the reality of purpose! Paul is saying that purpose has taken hold of him for something, yet he hasn't fully grasped all that it entails. Although he's been walking with God in purpose and accomplishing much, he knows he hasn't crossed the finish line. As a result, his lifetime commitment is to press on until he fulfills every aspect of what God saw for his life in the *before* realm. Later in the passage Paul speaks of how he forgets those things that are behind him and focuses his sights on the things that are ahead of him. He didn't want to get stuck in the last place that purpose had taken him. He realized that *who* he was would always be ahead of *where* he was. He understood that his purpose was evolving and wanted to always stay on course with it. This is the same mind-set you too must have to make the full scope of your purpose a reality.

Purpose Is a Living Organism

Your purpose is a life. It's not a part of your life—it is your life. Your purpose is the life that God designed for you. It's a living, breathing, and moving organism. Purpose walks, talks, thinks, makes decisions, learns, grows, and becomes everything that God saw beforehand. Purpose is never stagnant. It's alive and is always evolving. The objective of purpose is not simply to be discovered, but to be lived. This means that being awakened to purpose is just the beginning— becoming your purpose is the real objective. There's a point we must get to, where purpose goes from being very important to becoming our everything. At this level, it's the only thing you think or talk about. You are consumed by it. It captivates you and distracts you from all of life's distractions. As you evolve in your purpose awareness you'll come to realize that your life can't be lived any other way.

Your purpose is you—the real you, in eternal form. It's God's narrative about who you are and what your life is meant to be. It's an epic story with a glorious ending. As you evolve in your purpose, it makes you alive like never before. Purpose is life at its best. You are living out the very reason that brought you in to this world.

Your Purpose Guide

The evolution of your purpose happens as you are guided into the unfolding of God's plans for you. This guidance is not random or by happenstance but is achieved through divine communication and interaction. For example, let's consider our friend Abraham from earlier in the book. If you read his entire story, you'll discover that every successful step he took in purpose began as an instruction from above. God didn't leave Abraham to figure out his journey all by himself, and neither does He leave you to go at it alone. God remains very much involved in seeing His plan for you come together. When God designed your life's plan, He factored in a Helper, the Holy Spirit, to guide you on your way. This Helper's mission is to lead you, teach you, empower you, and motivate you on your path to purpose. God is so committed to you fulfilling His dream for you that He's made every provision necessary to ensure you are able to walk it out successfully. Your path is already paved, God Almighty has given His nod, and you have a personal purpose guide to make certain you arrive at your destination on schedule. You have been divinely set up to win.

Our purpose guide, the Holy Spirit, isn't a force, wind, or energy—He is a person with a personality. The Holy Spirit is your personal destiny advocate and the greatest proponent of your purpose you'll ever have. He is a committed confidant and a brilliant friend. He mentors, coaches, affirms, and encourages. He knows everything there is to know about your life and God's epic idea concerning it. What's amazing to me is that even though He embodies the fullness of God's mind and thoughts, He is fully knowable and longs to be in relationship with you. His purpose is to be your God-friend and to communicate to you the perspective of your purpose at any given moment. Furthermore, because He has already seen our end, He knows how to get us there with step-by-step instructions. He is so awesome that even when you make a wrong turn on your journey to purpose, the Holy Spirit, similar to a car's GPS system, will reroute you from where you are back onto the path of purpose.

The Holy Spirit communicates to us in many different ways. He speaks through sound, words, sight, images, thoughts, touch, and any other way He chooses to get a message across. What's important is not *how* He communicates to us, but what we feel and come to understand when He does. Remember, it's all spiritual; anything the Holy Spirit uses in the natural is for the purpose of revealing a spiritual truth. The Holy Spirit has access to the deepest parts of us. He knows us better than we know ourselves. He's got us figured out and knows the right time and the right spot within us to speak to us. When He communicates to us He bypasses our heads and goes straight to our hearts. He does this because He understands that our deepest convictions are held in our hearts—not in our heads.

As you grow in your relationship with the Holy Spirit you will start to become familiar with how He communicates to you. It's the same as it would be with any human relationship you may have. When you spend time with a person, you get accustomed to their ways. You learn their moods and their communication styles. You'll come to understand when they are pleased and when they are troubled. It's the same thing with the Holy Spirit. As with any other relationship, He can be pleased or grieved by our actions. One thing to always remember about the Holy Spirit is this—His only objective is to prosper you on your path to purpose. When you follow His leading and move in the right direction He is pleased and you can feel it within. You'll sense His approval and know that you are aligned with God's plan for your life. At other times you will feel grieved or like something isn't quite right. You may not be able to put your finger on it, but the freedom and the peace that you once had slip away. This too is from the Holy Spirit. The person of the Holy Spirit is a spirit just like you—only whole in every way. When you are in relationship with Him, what He feels, you'll feel also. This is to guide you on your path to purpose.

When the Holy Spirit is leading you on your path of purpose you will feel a great sense of wholeness. You'll know that you are right where you are supposed to be. The confirmation of peace will always be a key indicator that you are on the right track. It's a sign that you and your purpose guide are in unity. Remember, you are traveling a course that you have never been on before. The Holy Spirit, however, knows your path inside and out. When His peace becomes yours it means that you are in the center of God's will, and from that place you'll be catapulted forward into God's great plan.

Purpose Evolves as You Evolve

The evolution of your purpose works in conjunction with the evolution of you. As you evolve on your journey of purpose, your purpose itself will also evolve. The fullness of your purpose requires you to have certain capabilities in order to fulfill it. These capabilities involve knowledge, experience, wholeness, resources, and relationships. When you first begin on your path to purpose you will lack at least one of these things. Part of the function of the purpose journey is to cultivate the things needed to bring your capacity to the place that allows your purpose to be fulfilled.

I had no idea when I started my journey in purpose that my life would unfold to become what it has. And then to think that things are still evolving is mind-blowing to me. I've watched my purpose unfold and grow exponentially into something I could have never imagined from the start. My purpose went from me being spiritually enlightened to me becoming a minister in a church. It then evolved from me planting my own church of just a few people to growing it to hundreds. As my purpose continued to unfold even more, my voice became one that attracted many from young Hollywood, and the church grew into thousands. But wait, purpose didn't stop there. Next purpose took on a new shape with me creating state-of-the-art multimedia centers in L.A. to train creative people, while at the same time expanding the reach of the church to tens of thousands in over 150 nations. It gets better. My purpose then led me to take over and run a historic theater in Hollywood, and around the same time, purpose revealed to me that spreading God's message and joy via writing books was also part of God's plan for me.

The unfolding of my purpose has been an exhilarating experience so far, and there was absolutely no way I could see this from the start. Purpose, however, saw it from the gate, and my purpose guide knew exactly how to get me there. This is what purpose evolution looks like, but it couldn't have happened without its counterpart— the evolution of me.

The things I experienced at each phase in my purpose created the inner capacity I needed to take me to the next level of what God had for me. Each phase provided the training, lesson-learning, and character development to sustain me in the next phase of my purpose evolution. With each unfolding of my purpose, I increased in wisdom, knowledge, and character. I also gained experience in a wide variety of areas. I learned about myself—my strengths and my weaknesses—and I learned about other people too. I learned who I was, and, equally as important, I learned who I wasn't. I found out what my lane was, what worked for me and what didn't. I discovered the things I was ordained to do—the things that no one else could do but me.

Enduring the Process of Evolution

I want you to know—this wasn't always pretty. As a matter of fact, much of the experiences that increased my capacity along the way weren't situations that you would voluntarily enter into. Learning your weakness and what you are not good at usually involves some type of failure. Trust me, I had plenty. But the beautiful thing about God and His process of unfolding our purpose is that He provides safe places for us to make our mistakes. It's like the transformation process the caterpillar undergoes when becoming a butterfly. While it is in the process of evolution it is housed in the protection of the cocoon. The world can't see what's going on inside, but there is a whole lot that takes place. There are times in the cocoon when the butterfly-in-the-making is just a mass of mush. I don't know if you have ever experienced it, but there have been times when I felt like a big mass of mush. I remember times when I couldn't see how anything beautiful was going to emerge from the difficulty I was facing. I recall moments early on when I knew it was game over for sure. What I didn't realize then was that although my footing seemed to be unstable, God's protective cocoon hid me and kept me from falling. God knows that you fulfilling your purpose will require many levels of transformation. He allows certain situations to develop us in His cocoon, and when the time is right, He'll allow us to emerge as beautiful butterflies for the whole world to see.

Value Humble Beginnings

During my early days in purpose I wanted to rush to greatness overnight. I looked at great leaders and aspired to be like them without understanding what God had to develop *in* them to get them to where they were. I've since become much more patient with my ambition as my journey has taught me this valuable lesson. You've heard the saying "To whom much is given, much is required"? I'll echo that truth with a slight adjustment and say, "When much will be given, much development is first required." Don't be so quick to desire what the great have earned. It's a better option instead to desire what they've learned.

Another lesson I picked up during my purpose evolution was to appreciate humble beginnings. In hindsight, I'm thankful that our church remained small for several years. It was in these years that I made the majority of my significant mistakes. Had these same mistakes happened later in the evolution of our church it may have cost us everything. Oftentimes God will keep you in low-liability environments until your character and capacity aren't a threat to your future. Learn not to despise small beginnings. There is much purpose in what you may think is small or menial. If your path to purpose leads you to a humble place, embrace it, reflect while you are there, and gain the wisdom being afforded.

I remember a scene from the original *Karate Kid* movie. In the story, a young man wants to become great at martial arts and seeks out an instructor to train him. To the young man's surprise the teacher hands him a towel and tells him to start washing his cars. After a while the young man became frustrated, wondering what car washing had to do with martial arts. What he didn't realize was that the hand motions he was using to wash the cars were key fundamental movements in the martial art he was learning. These seemingly meaningless moves became the young man's foundation to becoming excellent at his craft. It may not always look like progress, but in purpose, everything is done for a reason. Each phase during the evolution of your purpose increases your capabilities for even greater things.

Turning the Wheels of Purpose

The evolution of purpose is similar to riding a bike. In order for a bike to move forward, both wheels have to turn. If we relate it to the evolution of purpose, one of the wheels on the bike represents your purpose. The other wheel represents you. If the wheel of purpose rotates forward but the wheel of you does not, the bike will go nowhere. But when both wheels are turning the bike moves forward and doesn't stop. This is how your life in purpose works. When you evolve, your purpose evolves; and when your purpose evolves, so do you. It all works hand in hand, and just like the bike, you will constantly move forward.

There is so much that God has in store for you. I've seen it first-hand in my own life. Your purpose is awesome and will always be evolving. Get to know your best friend on the path of purpose—the Holy Spirit. He will consistently answer the most important question on your journey: "What do I do next?" Once you get your instruction and follow it, you will be rewarded with success and accomplishment. You will soon realize that in purpose you can't fail. Even what looks like a setback is just preparing you for your upgrade. One day you will look back over your life and be completely amazed to see how something that started so small has evolved into amazing accomplishment.

Chapter 15

TROUBLE-SHOOTING PURPOSE

At this point you should be pretty fired up about the future God has waiting for you. Here's the awesome part—all you have to do is keep walking toward it and it's going to happen for you. So far I've talked about God's commitment to His epic plan for your life and all the provisions He's made toward you fulfilling it. We looked at Jesus, who destroyed everything that had power to hold you back from your destiny. We also discussed the Holy Spirit, your personal purpose guide who empowers you and leads you forward into God's plan for you. As we move deeper into the reality of your purpose, it is important for me to make you aware of another character you'll encounter on your journey. I wish I could say that this personality was an additional gift from God to help you out on your journey. The fact is, the exact opposite is true. This individual is the antithesis of God and of everything that represents good. Its mission is to distract you, discourage you, derail you from purpose, and ultimately destroy you. I know that's a lot to swallow, but it's something you've got to know. If I taught you about purpose and failed to mention what I'm sharing with you now it's quite possible everything you've learned up to this point could come to nothing in the end. This character is a relentless foe and is the root cause of great pain, loss, and havoc in people's lives. When the fullness of

God's epic idea for our world is complete nevertheless, this character won't even be remembered. But for now we have to learn how to navigate around this evil and overcome it for the sake of our destiny.

If God's nemesis wrote you a letter expressing the true intentions of his heart, this is how it would read:

For I know the plans I have for you. Plans to deceive you, harm you, and rob you of your future. My plan is to make you believe lies about yourself, your worth, your future, and your God. If I had my way I'd trick you and cause you to live hard and die fast. I would seduce you by telling you you're larger than life one day, and the next day make you feel so insignificant that you would want to die. Let me just cut to the chase; if I couldn't use you to perpetuate pain in the lives of others, I would encourage you to kill yourself. My plan is to rule you by fear and drive you by lust. Instead of healing your pain and brokenness, I would get you addicted to things that numb it, and then exploit you because of it. I would convince you to do things you didn't want to, and then turn around and condemn you for doing them. I would confuse you and get you to call good evil, and evil good. I would quickly separate you from anyone who is on to me, and especially keep you from truly knowing Jesus. I would keep you from knowing that I'm actually intimidated by the thought of you finding out who you really are. That's why I bring you endless philosophies and religions to distract you, instead of allowing you to discover Jesus and the power of what He has already done to free you from me. And because I can't stand the idea of you crossing the finish line of your purpose, my ultimate plan is to make you fall into a pit that you can never recover from.

If the liar had the capacity to tell you the truth, this is exactly what he would say.

It's not easy for me to be this direct with you. These words may even seem like they should have been in another book. This may even be a little scary for you. You may be thinking, "Wait a minute,

I don't want to know about all of this stuff. I just want to know why I'm here and how to discover my purpose in life. This is kind of a downer." I would totally understand if you felt this way. In fact, there is a reason why I waited until now to bring it up. I didn't bring it up sooner because evil should never be your focus when you are pursuing your purpose. You don't find your purpose by studying evil. However, an awareness of the evil around you will ensure that you stay on the course of your purpose, allowing you to accomplish it.

There is a term that describes the source and embodiment of all evil. It's a word that you are probably familiar with—*Satan*. The literal translation of this word means "one who obstructs or opposes." The reason why you can't afford to dismiss the idea of evil is because its job is to obstruct and oppose...guess what? Your purpose. The same way that the Holy Spirit is the biggest proponent of your purpose and is committed to guiding you there—Satan is the biggest *opponent* of everything about you and is literally *hell-bent* on obstructing your path to purpose.

Your Purpose Has a Hater

When I became an adult, I discovered something significant that happened in my past which now makes sense as I consider what my purpose is today. I learned that when my mother found out she was pregnant with me and told my father, there was an ultra-brief discussion about her having an abortion. This conversation was over in two seconds, but in hindsight I realize this was one of the obstructer's first attempts at destroying my purpose. Before I could even make it out of the womb there was an assassination attempt on my life. This reveals how relentless our foe is and how low he will go to sabotage our destiny. Thankfully that scheme came to nothing and quite a lovely baby boy was born. But that would be just the first of many schemes and strategies he would use to attempt to derail me from the very things I am doing today.

Check out this passage that shows Satan doing his job well:

Then he showed me Joshua the high priest standing before the Angel of the LORD, and Satan standing at his right hand to oppose him. (Zechariah 3:1)

In this passage a guy named Joshua is standing in the presence of God getting ready to step into his purpose and fulfill his destiny. And of course, at that very moment you-know-who shows up with one objective—to oppose and obstruct what is getting ready to happen in Joshua's life. It doesn't quite work out the way the adversary planned. If you keep reading the story, God exercises His supremacy over Satan by rebuking him and ultimately telling him to get lost. Satan immediately disappears from the scene, and the story ends with God telling Joshua the details of his future. Clearly Satan lost the battle for that day, but my own experiences make me pretty confident that Joshua would have to face him again.

What Starts Bad Can End Good

Sixteen years after escaping the threat of death in my mother's womb I came face to face with death again. This time I would become an innocent victim of a drive-by shooting, an epidemic that had become so common in the inner city that the authorities gave it a name reminiscent of something you'd expect to find at a fast-food restaurant. It was a difficult time in Los Angeles, and many families faced much pain and grief. So many innocent victims lost their lives, and I myself came close to being one of them.

I still remember that night. I was driving with another teenager when a truck full of men pulled alongside of us. One of the men emerged from the back of the truck, pulled out a large handgun, and began shooting directly into my car. Everything was happening in slow motion. I remember seeing the look on the shooter's face.

He had no emotion at all. It was evil in pure form. He was like a human shell with no heart and soul. Here I was, a sixteen-year-old kid, but it didn't matter to him. This killer was determined to end my life that night. He pointed the gun toward my head and opened fire. One bullet nearly struck me in the head, shattering the window just behind me. He took his time, aimed his gun, and fired over and over again. I remember feeling trapped with no place to escape. What happened next can only be described as what felt like someone taking a sledgehammer, throwing it over their shoulder, walking backward fifty paces, then charging full steam toward me and swinging the hammer at me, striking me in the upper torso. The pain alone sent my body into shock. Inside my body I could feel the extreme heat and fire from the bullet. Before long I was lying on the ground with a bullet in my body, coughing up blood and seeing my life flash before my eyes. I thought I was going to die. Once again the obstructer tried his hand, this time even more vehemently, at keeping God's epic plan for my life from being realized. I mean evil threw its best shot at me—pun intended—but still came up short.

You've probably figured out by now that I didn't die. In fact, I experienced a supernatural healing that puzzled the doctors who treated me. What's even more awesome is that instead of this situation scarring me for life, it made me more passionate about discovering my purpose. I thought to myself, "If my destiny is being so violently opposed by evil, then how extraordinarily *good* must it really be?" If Satan would go through so much trouble to try and end my life before I was awakened to purpose, then there must be something profoundly significant about the future of the man I see every day in the mirror. What may have been seen as a tragic event in my life was actually one of the very things that God would use to thrust me into my destiny. It's amazing what God can do!

Now you might be thinking, "Hold on here—that's a great story with a happy ending and all, but I don't want to have to get shot to be motivated toward my purpose." I can appreciate how you feel, and if there's any consolation in this—just know that most people don't have to get shot to discover their purpose. I would never suggest that my story has to be yours, and quite frankly I pray that you'll endure far less for the sake of fulfilling your destiny. What I am saying, however, is that the fulfilling of your purpose will definitely require you to overcome certain scenarios that the obstructer will place before you on your path to purpose.

But even when opposition arises, know this. Before the Almighty God will allow the obstructer to place an obstacle in your path, He has already prequalified you to handle it and has given you the strength to overcome it. God will only allow things on your path that He knows will ultimately work toward helping you to fulfill His epic idea for you. Not only will you be endowed with the strength to come out victorious, but you'll be better off than you were before the opposition arose.

The Two Most Common Strategies That Sabotage Purpose

Although the obstructer hardly runs short of creative ways to attempt to keep us from our destiny, I have identified the two common strategies that are most often used. Once you are able to recognize them, you'll be able to sidestep time-consuming derailments and swiftly move forward down the path of your purpose.

The Lie of Inadequacy

One of the primary things Satan uses to derail us from purpose is to instill in us a sense of inadequacy. He understands that we can never accomplish beyond how we see ourselves. The obstructer's assault always begins with an attack on how we perceive ourselves. It starts up close and personal. It whispers lies about you. It's the voice that tells you what you can't do. It brings up your mistakes and failures and defines you by them. It blackmails you with the mistakes of your past and disqualifies you from the prospects of your future. When you start to dream, he swiftly brings to your recollection why you are the least qualified for the future God is promising. You would be surprised to discover how many great people in history struggled with a sense of inadequacy. Almost every significant figure in Scripture wrestled with it from time to time. Let's peek into one of those accounts. This passage shows even the great prophet Jeremiah struggling with inadequacy when God approached him to reveal his great future.

> *The word of the LORD came to me, saying, "Before I formed you in the womb I knew you, before you were born I set you apart; I appointed you as a prophet to the nations."*
>
> *"Alas, Sovereign LORD," I said, "I do not know how to speak; I am too young."*
>
> *But the LORD said to me, "Do not say, 'I am too young.' You must go to everyone I send you to and say whatever I command you. Do not be afraid of them, for I am with you and will rescue you," declares the LORD. (Jeremiah 1:4–8 NIV)*

In this passage there is an exchange between God and Jeremiah. God approaches Jeremiah, proclaims his identity, and predicts his future. Jeremiah is immediately gripped with a sense of inadequacy and begins to reject the identity and destiny that God had just spoken of. It was clear at that moment that Jeremiah's view of himself was much less than what God knew about him. This happens so often to us in life. Most people will always have a view of themselves and their capabilities that is far less than what God sees. Where did this way of thinking come from? Without question, it came from Satan. Another translation of the word Satan is *accuser*. In Scripture he is referred to as the accuser of mankind. This is his job, and he is good at it. When a person feels accused, guilty, or less than, it makes them more likely to become someone's slave—and more specifically, a slave of the one who is making the accusation. This is not the way God motivates people to serve Him. He doesn't use fear to motivate us—He uses love. It's His kindness, not a guilt trip, that leads us to turn toward Him.

In the passage Jeremiah struggles with seeing himself right, but God doesn't allow him to stay there. When Jeremiah begins to disqualify himself in inadequacy, God interrupts his self-degrading speech. God realized that Jeremiah was sabotaging his destiny with his own words. Sometimes in life the accuser can have you so convinced that you are inadequate that he doesn't even have to say it anymore—you start saying it yourself. With your own words you can destroy your own destiny. There is so much power in what you say. Your words create your world. You must always make certain that your words work for you and not against you. It's the same with your mind. Your mind is meant to be a tool that serves the purpose and the vision of your life. It should motivate you, not discourage you.

God comes right back at Jeremiah and begins to reinforce the truth about his future. He tells Jeremiah to change his speech, for he indeed was every bit of who God said he was, and would accomplish everything that God had promised.

When God speaks, you must always listen for your identity in what He says. He's the only one who knows who you truly are and what you are capable of. After all, He's the One who made you. He doesn't speak to you beyond your ability, He speaks to you according to what your ability actually is. If God says you're the one, regardless of the task, you are more than able to accomplish it.

Recognizing Distraction

The other thing that you will have to avoid on your path of purpose is distraction. Distractions are tricky, because you don't realize you've been distracted until after the fact. I was amazed once by how much work I was able to get accomplished in a short amount of time simply by turning off my iPhone. It was paradise. But that experience also communicated to me a painful truth. It suggested that I spend the majority of my life at least a little bit distracted. If you think about it, our entire economy is built upon distractions. When you sit down to watch your favorite sitcom, you're not signing up for the fast food presentation that will come on like clockwork. They pay top dollar to the network you're watching for permission to distract you. Advertising firms make big bucks on billboards designed to draw your attention away from whatever you intended to be looking at and toward what they want to sell you. And guess what—it works. We are such a distracted society. We've got phone calls, emails, text messages, tweets, and Facebook, along with a whole new suite of things on the horizon, all designed to accost our focus.

Wouldn't it be cool if some sort of alarm or warning system went off the next time something was getting ready to distract you? It would be awesome if the next time someone called and interrupted you from what you were doing, the caller ID showed "DISTRACTION—DO NOT ANSWER." That would be nice, but unfortunately it isn't reality. This means we have to set up our own warning systems to keep us from being distracted from progressing in our purpose.

Remember, Satan is a very strategic opponent. He knows that all you have to do is stay focused on your purpose, and with the Holy Spirit's help, you'll be successful. He lives to prevent this from happening and will commission many non-purpose-related activities to draw your attention away. Believe it or not, the cure for distraction is simple—it's focus. Purpose requires concentration. It mandates that we set goals and objectives daily, and stick to them. Purpose requires that we qualify every activity in our lives. No time or situation should be random, and everything should have meaning. Even if you decide to spend the day resting or doing nothing at all, it should still be according to what the purpose of your life is.

One last thought on the subject of distraction that I think will be helpful to you. The obstructer often reserves his greatest distraction for the moment just before you make a major accomplishment in your purpose. There has never failed to be some sort of last-minute bombshell dropped as I am on the cusp of a significant destiny breakthrough. From family issues to unexpected financial hurdles to technology challenges—sometimes even all of them happening at once. I'm hardly surprised when the storm comes right before the breaking of a new day. I don't say this to alarm you—just to make you aware. The key is to know where it's coming from when it's happening and that God has already made a way for you to overcome and finish strong.

I want to leave you with a promise from God in the Scripture that helps us to understand that we have victory in all things—even from the obstructer himself.

> *Every test that you have experienced is the kind that normally comes to people. But God keeps his promise, and he will not allow you to be tested beyond your power to remain firm; at the time you are put to the test, he will give you the strength to endure it, and so provide you with a way out. (1 Corinthians 10:13 GNT)*

God has already gone ahead of you and made a way for your success. His epic plan for you has already considered every giant you will face and every obstacle you will encounter. When he built you, He placed inside you everything you'd need to carry out your assignment. You are the right one for the job and have an incredible destiny waiting for you. Nothing can stop you. There's nothing strong enough to prevent you from winning. If things get challenging, pause and reflect. Then get right back in the race because you have already been ordained to win.

Part VI

WALKING IT OUT

Chapter 16

YOUR PURPOSE MATE

When God ponders who you will be and what His epic plans are for your life, He also considers what people He'll use to help you to accomplish it. There will always be others assigned to the epic idea that motivated your birth. Purpose doesn't place you on an island of independence; it guarantees you will have to connect with others to make it a reality. God's epic idea for your life is so much bigger than what you can pull off by yourself. It will take the involvement and resources of others that will appear along your path to fulfill what God has started in you. Your purpose is intertwined with the purposes of others, and it's an amazing moment when two people "accidentally" figure that out.

One day I received a message from my assistant saying that there was a young lady who wanted to meet with me to discuss the possibility of being my manager. At the time I figured I was doing a good job of managing myself and didn't quite understand how a manager could benefit me. Nevertheless, I was curious so I took the meeting. Once we got past the small talk, the young lady began to nervously present her pitch to be my manager. As she spoke my *purpose guide* came alive and the Holy Spirit instructed me to simply listen. Her words began to cut right to my heart. She said things that reached to the core of me and pulled to the surface desires that were buried deep inside my heart. I sat there in awe. Not only was her vision the exact vision I had for my future, but she had a clear strategy on how to get me there. I was blown away. Three mind-boggling questions immediately arose in my mind: (1) How could this stranger be so in tune with the dreams that were in my heart? (2) How could she have all of the resources I needed to make these dreams come true? (3) Out of all of the people on the planet, how could my path cross with someone who not only had understanding of my dreams and the resources needed, but the desire to help me manifest these dreams? It was a surreal moment. The answer to these questions was simple—she was a purpose mate that God had assigned to my life.

Faith + Humility = Breakthrough

One way to determine whether or not a person in your life is a purpose mate is the fruit that the relationship bears. It would have been a false alarm if my would-be manager all of a sudden fell off the map, or later proved that she was all talk and couldn't deliver. In this case the opposite was true. Within sixty days of working together I had my first book deal with a major publisher and was well on my way to becoming a published author. As a matter of fact, the book that you are reading right now is proof of both the reality and the power of the purpose mates that are assigned to your life. Trust me, yours are out there too. They could be in your life right now, but you have to learn how to recognize and manage those relationships. I'm going to talk about this in more detail, but now I want to look at my initial encounter with this purpose mate to point out some helpful tips. In this interaction there were a couple of things that went right. Let's look at them.

First of all, the young lady asserted herself and asked for the meeting. It had to have been intimidating for her to step out on a limb and approach a very busy executive seeking to manage him, but she had the faith to do it. I'm sure there were doubts and fears she had to overcome to do so. Had she given in to those doubts and fears she would have been robbed of a purpose encounter and all that would come out of it. The lesson here is to never be afraid to put yourself out there, especially if you feel the Holy Spirit is leading you. The worst thing someone can say is no, which involves no real risk on your part. The alternative, however, could be something that changes the course (and the finances) of your life forever.

The second thing to take from the story is the fact that I had the humility to take the meeting. I wasn't short of calendar items at the time, but something within instructed me to make time for this meeting. There is little that will take you further in life than learning to honor, respect, and serve people—especially the ones who seemingly can't add value to your life. I didn't know this young lady from Eve. She didn't have a big name nor did she represent a huge firm. I took the meeting because of her consistency in reaching out to me. Had I been too much of a big shot to sit down with her, I would have missed an opportunity of a lifetime. It's a wise thing to never discredit or disregard someone based on what you feel they haven't accomplished. It may be the case that God has reserved their greatest accomplishments to be done in collaboration with you. The greatest miracles often come in unassuming packages; therefore always be humble enough to consider the best about everyone you come into contact with.

The Value of Collaboration

There are so many things that purpose mates add to each other's lives. These relationships always complement one another and are mutually beneficial. Purpose mates pull purpose out of you. They have keys that unlock your purpose potential. If I had never met my manager, my desire to write books would have remained within. An author was trapped inside of me needing a purpose mate to show up and let him out. God has orchestrated things in a way that causes us to rely on each other, even to fulfill our destinies. God loves collaboration. He wouldn't even allow the first man, Adam, to step into his destiny before introducing him to Eve, his first purpose mate. Check out this passage from Genesis.

> *Then the LORD God said, "It is not good for the man to live alone. I will make a suitable companion to help him." Then the LORD God made the man fall into a deep sleep, and while he was sleeping, he took out one of the man's ribs and closed up the flesh. He formed a woman out of the rib and brought her to him. Then the man said, "At last, here is one of my own kind—Bone taken from my bone, and flesh from my flesh. 'Woman' is her name because she was taken out of man." (Genesis 2:18, 21–23 GNT)*
>
> *So God created man in His own image; in the image of God He created him; male and female He created them. Then God blessed them, and God said to them, "Be fruitful and multiply; fill the earth and subdue it; have dominion over the fish of the sea, over the birds of the air, and over every living thing that moves on the earth." (NKJV Genesis 1:27–28)*

This is such a fascinating story with so many implications. First of all, Eve represents Adam's potential. When God originally made man, He did so with the woman inside of him. In a sense, Adam was pregnant with Eve but didn't know it. There was more to him than he realized. There was capacity on the inside of him that he was unaware of. Then God, knowing that in order for Adam to realize the full potential of his destiny, would need to manifest what was inside of him. Next, God puts Adam to sleep, reaches inside of him, and brings forth not only his potential, but his purpose mate, Eve. Adam being put to sleep represents the fact that the manifesting of your purpose mate isn't something that you can manufacture. This is something that only God can do. Adam had no involvement in bringing Eve forth, but was there to acknowledge her and receive the blessing she brought to him when he woke from his sleep. Once this happened they were released into the great purpose that God had assigned to them.

Your purpose mate is your potential, and every time you encounter one, not only will your life be enhanced, but another dimension of your purpose will open up to you.

The Characteristics of a Purpose Mate

There are four key characteristics of the purpose mates who are assigned to your life. You should be able to identify a purpose mate by at least one of these things.

1. **They Encourage Your Purpose:** True purpose mates will be as excited about your purpose as you are. You don't have to fire up purpose mates about your purpose—they already are. These people encourage your dreams. When you want to throw in the towel and quit, they won't let you. They believe in you and go out of their way to motivate you toward fulfilling your purpose in life.

2. **They Take Your Purpose to the Next Level:** Purpose mates add a dimension to your purpose that you didn't even know existed. They add detail and color to the dreams you have. Your vision is expanded by the input they give you. Collaborating with them takes your visions from great to amazing.

3. **They Facilitate Your Purpose:** These purpose mates have the resources and/or the relationships that allow your purpose to happen. These are influential people whom God brings into your life that believe in your vision. They are fulfilled as they use what God has given them, to help you fulfill what God has given you to do.

4. **They Stimulate Your Purpose:** Lastly, there are purpose mates who stimulate your thoughts and ideas about your purpose. These are people who activate creativity in you. You only need to

be around them a short time and your vision crystallizes. You always leave their presence motivated; ready to take on the world if necessary to make your vision a reality.

These key characteristics are vital qualifiers concerning who you allow to walk with you on your purpose journey. God will always make sure there are people in your life who aid you in these ways. One thing to remember, however, is that if you have the wrong people in key positions in your life, it prevents the right people from showing up. Take inventory of who's around you and make certain that they are purpose mates. If they are not, then put a space between you and them. Make the space wide enough to allow the true purpose mates to have a place in your life. Who you walk with on the journey, and who you allow to walk with you, will make all the difference in the world. God's got an awesome plan for you, and He has placed great people out there to help you carry it out.

Managing Purpose Mate Relationships

Your relationships with your purpose mates are the most important relationships you'll ever have. For this reason you must be diligent to take care of them. Don't make the mistake of thinking that these relationships will take care of themselves. This simply is not true. Purpose mates are not perfect—they are human beings just like all of us. They have cares, needs, issues, and concerns. They are just as challenged in life at times as we are. They have insecurities and fears to overcome, just like everyone else on their journey to wholeness. It's important to invest time with your purpose mates and always build upon that relationship. Don't assume that everything is fine with them. Check on them from time to time, and when you do, don't even mention your purpose. Be genuinely concerned about them and seek ways to serve them. Think about it—this is your partner. It's to your advantage to make sure they're doing well in every way. As they prosper, so will you, and you'll both cross the finish line God has set for you.

Purpose mate relationships are vital to fulfilling your purpose in life, and as a result they often become targets of the obstructer. He will go after these relationships to try to divide them, and if they aren't being tended to, he can succeed. Always keep the communication lines open. If there is a conflict, talk it through. Never leave words unspoken and work to create an atmosphere in the relationship that promotes transparency and honesty. Instead of pointing out your purpose mate's flaws, strive to be the best that *you* can be. Embrace humility and consider your partner just as honorable, if not more, than yourself. Never receive a negative report about your purpose mate that you don't discuss with them to get their side. Believe in them and always focus on their best qualities. Be honest with yourself and deal with jealousy or competitiveness when it tries to creep in. Remember, their success is your success. If you will diligently appreciate and manage your purpose mate relationships, you will greatly maximize the potential that relationship brings.

Keeping Purpose in the Relationship

When God brings a purpose mate into your life, it's for a specific reason. If the relationship is maintained in the context of the original idea, it will be a mutually beneficial situation. The moment that the relationship starts to veer away from the original intention, it is headed for danger and ineffectiveness. Relationships should always have context or some definition to them. I've made the costly mistake in the past of misidentifying the role people were to play in my life, and every time I did it turned into a disaster. It is critical to know what roles people are to play in your life and for how long. Ask the Holy Spirit on a regular basis, "What role is this person to play in my life and mine in theirs?" Once you have an answer in your heart, stick to it and remain within the boundaries of what you heard.

I've seen people who were supposed to be purpose mates wrongly enter into romantic relationships. Now, I'm not saying that a purpose mate can't be a mate-mate. In fact, your mate-mate needs to be your purpose mate or that relationship is doomed to fail. What I'm saying is, at times the original intention of a relationship can get perverted and become something that God never intended. This will cause what He *did* intend to be aborted. You must strive to always see the relationship in the right way. Purpose mate relationships can easily become distracted. Stay focused and remember the reason why you are in each other's lives. I don't mean you have to be so rigid that you can't relax around each other. I simply mean that there's a priority in the relationship that you must protect. It can't be jeopardized and must be upheld by all means. After all, your purpose is depending on it.

Purpose and Marriage

Who you marry is one of the most important decisions you'll ever make in life. Marriage is a huge blessing and is designed to enhance life in a way that no other relationship can. However, marriage is never something that should be taken lightly or rushed into. It requires much prayer, contemplation, and counsel to even decide that this is the direction you want to move in. Once that has been determined, there should be a comprehensive pre-marriage plan to prepare the bride and groom for the life they have chosen to share together. If they make it through this process, then they can plan for the actual wedding. You may be thinking, "Wow, that seems to be a bit much." I would agree with you. It is much. But when you are talking about committing yourself to someone for the rest of your life, you must make sure that this person is the one who has been chosen for you.

Everything in life has purpose, even who you decide to marry. As a spiritual leader who often counsels couples who are considering marriage, I make it a point to make one thing clear. You shouldn't even consider marrying anyone unless you know what your purpose in life is. Now this might seem a little harsh, but it's very true. If you heed these words it could keep you from a great deal of pain in the future.

To marry is to say to someone, "I am giving myself to you for life and you are giving yourself to me." But what happens when you don't know yourself well enough to know who you are giving to the other person? To marry without knowing your purpose in life could cause your spouse to one day wake up to a stranger, simply because you discovered who you are. And what happens when you realize that who you are is no longer relevant to who your spouse is; and who your spouse is isn't relevant to the purpose that you've been awakened to? One of two things will happen in these cases. Either you will surrender your purpose for the sake of the marriage, or you will be forced to endure the painful process of surrendering your marriage for the sake of your purpose. On occasion, with counsel, the right resources, and God's help, things can be salvaged. But for the most part you'll fall in one direction or the other. None of these scenarios are fun or ideal, and that is the reason why you must find out who you truly are before deciding to bond for life.

You don't have to rush any relationship, whether romantic or otherwise. What God has for you is for you. You will never miss out on the right thing waiting for the confirmation of purpose. God's got you covered. When you are aligned with your purpose, everything that is connected to it will appear at just the right time.

You don't need to seek out your purpose mate. Now, there's nothing wrong with praying for the right people to enter your life; as a matter of fact, I encourage that. But make sure that *you* are not the one seeking them out. Resist the temptation to manipulate circumstances to attract someone you think can help with your purpose. Remember, who God is choosing to help your purpose may be someone you would never even consider. God has already calculated everything you'll need to bring the vision of your purpose to reality.

All you have to do is stay aligned, continue listening to your purpose guide, and you will attract the right people to your life. These will be your purpose mates, some for a season, and some for a lifetime. No matter their duration in your life, you'll be better because they showed up. These are your teammates on your marathon of purpose, and with their help you'll be able to finish strong.

Chapter 17

FINISHING WELL

Surely you know that many runners take part in a race, but only one of them wins the prize. Run, then, in such a way as to win the prize. Every athlete in training submits to strict discipline, in order to be crowned with a wreath that will not last; but we do it for one that will last forever. That is why I run straight for the finish line; that is why I am like a boxer who does not waste his punches. I harden my body with blows and bring it under complete control, to keep myself from being disqualified after having called others to the contest. (1 Corinthians 9:24–27 GNT)

It's amazing the lengths God goes through to make certain we have everything needed to finish the course our purpose sets us on. God gives us vision, wisdom, tools, ability, and even a purpose guide to lead us on our path. He gives us the resources and relationships needed to accomplish the tasks at hand, but there's one thing He will not do. He'll never run your race for you. Even with all of God's equipping and preparing, you still must run your own race and finish the course that has been laid before you. The fulfillment of the epic idea that motivated your birth requires your initiative. To finish your race strong you've got to want it more than anything else in life. You've got to see the incomparable value of your purpose and be willing to attain it, no matter the cost.

The Necessity of Character

To be honest with you—finishing the course is much different from starting. The further you get on your journey to purpose, the more demands the course places on your character. In fact, much of what you experience on your journey to purpose is to develop your character. Your character is the thing that will determine just how far you go on the path of purpose. It's the main thing that determines whether you finish well or not. Character is widely defined as who you are when no one is looking. It's your inner self, and it determines the outcomes of your life. Although a person's character is within, the fruit of that character will show up outside. It's impossible to separate a person from his or her character. All you have to do is give people time and you will discover what their true character is like. I make it a point to observe people who enter my life for a period of time before giving them significant access to me. I call this period of time "the four seasons." The thought behind this is that it usually takes observing people's character a full round of seasons before you can determine what type of fruit they will bear. When things are good, how do they behave? In difficult times, who do they become? In summer they can appear to be an orange tree, but come winter the truth reveals they actually only produce lemons. Take the time to qualify people who show up in your life for an entire cycle of seasons. This way you can be certain of who they really are.

God's desire is to shape our character in a way that guarantees we not only manage our purpose well, but can finish our race strong. Remember, when it comes to purpose, it's not how you begin that matters, but how you finish.

Running Your Race to Win It

In the passage at the beginning of this chapter, our friend Paul is sharing with us the trade secrets about his character that would assure that he finished his race well. The first thing he tells us is that he's running the race to win it. He distinguishes himself from every other runner by saying that many people run, but only one turns up with the prize. This is a reminder to us that our commitment to fulfilling the purpose of our lives shouldn't have anything to do with the commitment levels of others around us. It's not uncommon to experience people, sometimes even friends, who might be running their race but not with the determination to win it. These types of people have a lackluster approach to purpose and as a result will just barely make it across the finish line, if at all. Now I'm not saying it's your job to go around judging other people's commitment to their purpose race, because you won't ever know all that God is doing in their lives. What I do mean, however, is that your responsibility is to run your race, and it must be run with a winner's mind-set and resolve.

There will be times when you'll have to break out from the pack of the ordinary and the uncommitted to keep from losing the momentum needed to finish your race strong. This is hardly an easy thing to do, but it has to happen. If you are not careful, the energy of the other runners will begin to affect your race. You'll get around certain people and instead of feeling energized for your race, you'll feel drained of energy. This is because energies are interactive. People were made to be in relationship with one another. We affect each other every day with the energy that we emit. If you are full of passion and drive, and you walk into a room filled with people in hopelessness and despair, one of three scenarios will take place: (1) those who were depressed and in despair will feed off of the energy you just brought to the room and become uplifted, (2) you will lose some of the passion and commitment you had when you walked in the room, or (3) you quickly make a U-turn and leave that room altogether to maintain your momentum.

The energy of others *will* affect you. In scenario one there was a positive outcome, which is great. The only thing is, it costs you energy and focus. You had to take your focus off of your race and give your energy to the room. That is always a wonderful thing to do, as long as you aren't distracted from or too drained to run your own race. Scenario two is absolutely out of the question. Your energy is a gift from God, and you can't let any environment siphon it. You can get around people you're trying to help and before you know it, you are completely drained without them being helped in any lasting way. Scenario three will be the one you'll need to employ the most in your effort to finish your race strong. You should encourage people and do your best to motivate them to run their race, but always remember—you can't run it for them. They have to want to win their race just as badly as you want to win yours. If not, they are going to slow you down. Paul reminds us that in order to finish strong, we must run our race in such a way that winning is the only outcome.

The Discipline of Self-Discipline

Why do so many people find it hard to be disciplined? The answer is simple. It's because discipline takes self-initiative and self-mastery. Any time you see the word *self* in front of any phrase, you can guarantee that it will take commitment to realize. On the other hand, when someone else is watching or we have to give an account to a superior, all of a sudden we are magically inclined to commit to a thing. The truth is, our standards for ourselves are often lower when it comes to things that will not matter to other people. Let me give you an example. If there were no outer benefits to working out— no six packs, no weight loss, and no tight buns—half of the world's fitness centers would go out of business. It's true! Of course you've got those of us who know that it's more than just looking good, it's about health and being fit; but surely even we enlightened ones would work out differently, perhaps even less, if no one could see the results.

In the passage Paul speaks of submitting himself to strict discipline so he could obtain an imperishable crown that was waiting for him. You can feel his determination by the passion with which he speaks. He's got a clear picture of what's awaiting him at the finish line, values its worth, and is fully committed to seeing it come to fruition. This lets us know that the type of discipline needed to finish our race strong requires motivation and focus.

Discipline has a price tag. It costs something. You will only pay for something that has value to you. You will only be as disciplined as the value you place on fulfilling your purpose and finishing strong. Your purpose in life has to be the thing that you value the most. It must be seen as your life—the very thing you were born for. To live a life outside of it is to live as an imposter to your own self. Purpose is so critical that if you don't know what the purpose of your life is, your purpose in life becomes to discover it.

When you understand that there is an epic plan behind your existence—something that has never been seen or heard of before; an amazing idea that is specific to your life only—it motivates you to bring your entire being into a posture that moves you directly toward it. You are focused like never before. You've got passion and zeal. You become determined to see it manifest, and you'll be consistent in the disciplines that will get you there.

Be Excellent

There's another trade secret that Paul lets us in on. He reveals to us his commitment to excellence. He compares himself to a disciplined boxer who doesn't waste any punches. When you consider a boxer in a fight, he must use his energy wisely. There is purpose in all of his movements. Every punch has an intention. He doesn't waste one. He realizes that his energy level will only account for a certain amount of swings. This means that he's got to make every single punch count. He doesn't recklessly and randomly throw out wild punches. He's focused, he's disciplined, and he's excellent.

When you realize there is an epic idea hovering above your life, you begin to embrace a lifestyle of excellence. You no longer do random things of mediocrity and insignificance. You are now identifying with who you truly are, and everything that you endeavor to do, you now do in excellence. Your standards for your time and activities are high. When you are asked to perform a task or be a part of something, the first things you consider are: (1) Is this in my purpose? and (2) Will it be excellent? If the answer is no to either question, you gracefully decline. Remember, you aren't wasting any punches. When you swing at something it has to strike right in the bull's-eye of excellence. Everything with your name on it from now on should be associated with excellence. It is better to wait on the opportunity to do something excellent than to be a part of something mediocre.

The people of Jesus' generation commended Him by saying, "He did all things well." They weren't speaking solely of the things that were regarded as "spiritual." Everything He did, He did in excellence, because excellence was who He was. If you are someone's employee, work in excellence. If you are a student, be disciplined and prepare your work with excellence. If you are an entrepreneur, your excellence will be your distinction from your competitors. Even if you are a volunteer, work with the level of excellence you would give if the position paid you billions. It may just lead you to such an opportunity. Your excellence attracts excellent things to you. Your excellence puts you on a frequency that summons all of the excellent things that are assigned to your purpose. It's like the old adage "when the student is ready, the teacher will appear." When you are committed to a lifestyle of excellence, epic things await you.

Regulating Self

Of all the disciplines we have to use to finish what God puts in us, there is none more key than the discipline of self-control. Remember, our journey to wholeness is about being transformed from a limited and deficient old self into a new self, fully enabled to manifest God's epic plan for our life. The catch is, this full transformation doesn't happen overnight. There is a lifelong process of becoming that takes place, that won't be complete until we are standing face to face, fully perfected in the presence of God. This means that while we are in the process of changing, we have to learn how to allow our renewed self to bring our old self under subjection. We still have old ways of thinking that haven't been renewed. If we allow ourselves to think the old thoughts we will find ourselves in some of the old actions. The key here is to continue to renew our minds with the new thoughts and ideas that our transformation brings to us. We have to be quick to replace any thought that doesn't guide us toward God's epic plan with those that do.

Understanding Temptation

Another thing that self-control will help you to do is win the battle against temptation. How you respond to temptation is key to whether or not you finish your course well. As a matter of fact, the purpose of temptation is to throw you off course, but it doesn't have to, and I'm going to show you how.

There are many misunderstandings about temptation that I want to address. The first misunderstanding I want to clear up is to make you aware that temptation is not sin. Let's look at a passage that defines and describes what temptation really is:

Blessed is the man who endures temptation; for when he has been approved, he will receive the crown of life which the Lord has

*promised to those who love Him. But each one is tempted when he
is drawn away by his own desires and enticed. Then, when desire
has conceived, it gives birth to sin; and sin, when it is full-grown,
brings forth death. (James 1:12, 14–15)*

This passage is the most revelatory you'll ever find on the subject
of temptation. There's so much wisdom here. It starts out by saying
there's actually a blessing for the person who endures temptation.
The Greek word that is often translated *temptation* is the word *peiras-
mos* (pi-ras-mos'). This word literally means "a putting to proof."
This means that the only thing temptation is supposed to do in your
life is to prove that you are who you truly are. One of the best feelings in the world is when you are tempted by something a part of
you desires, but the real you shows up and chooses to resist it. This
proves to you that your life has changed; that you aren't who you
used to be, and that with God's help you are unstoppable. When we
learn to get out of our own way, there'll be no limits to what we can
do. Always know that temptation isn't sin—it's just the presentation
of a choice. It's an opportunity to choose well and be greatly blessed
as a result.

Another misconception about temptation is that it is too strong
for you to resist. This notion also isn't true. Let's look at another passage on temptation:

*No temptation has overtaken you except what is common to man-
kind. And God is faithful; he will not let you be tempted beyond
what you can bear. But when you are tempted, he will also provide
a way out so that you can endure it. (1 Corinthians 10:13 NIV)*

Every temptation that you are faced with comes with an *optional*
escape route. I emphasize the word *optional* because, well—it's optional. God won't force you to take it, but He wants you to know
that it's there. Why? Because many people believe that if they are
confronted with temptation they have no defense against it and *must*

succumb to it. This is untrue, and if you believe it, it will become your reality. You can win the battle of any temptation that comes to you by yielding yourself to the part of you that has been renewed and is passionate about your purpose.

At the end of the day, temptation is simply desire. The remedy is to have more desire for your destiny than you do for what's distracting you from it. It's a desire game, and you have to master it. It's not so much about what temptation is trying to draw you *toward*, the greater concern is about what temptation is trying to draw you away *from*.

There is a place you can get to in your zeal for God's plan, where the idea of anything that would take you from it becomes absurd. What you are calling temptation today will be nothing more than a preposterous proposition once you get on fire for your purpose.

Overcoming Temptation

In order to be equipped to win the battle against temptation you must understand how it works. Let's revisit the first passage we looked at on temptation:

> *But each one is tempted when he is drawn away by his own desires and enticed. Then, when desire has conceived, it gives birth to sin; and sin, when it is full-grown, brings forth death.*

Here's how temptation works. When a person is tempted, they are being drawn away from their purpose by something within. There is no other way to say this than to tell you point blank—you have a *purpose sabotager* within you. This isn't to make you feel bad or to think less of yourself, it's just to let you know what you're up against. When you think about it, it's really no secret. We've all been stupefied at least once in our lives and found ourselves shaking our head asking the infamous question, "What in the world made me do that?" The answer is simple. It's the enemy within, and it must be subdued to keep us from sabotaging our future. The good news is that the true you is stronger than the anti-you, and you can learn to overcome any temptation.

The Seven Phases of Temptation

The process of temptation plays out with these seven steps:

1. **You are drawn.** This is when you are distracted from your purpose and pulled away.
2. **You are enticed.** Something within you is connecting with the temptation.
3. **The desire is conceived.** This happens when you come into agreement with the temptation.
4. **Sin is birthed.** You purpose to act on what you've agreed to or go through with it.
5. **No repentance happens.** You aren't remorseful and fail to acknowledge the wrong.
6. **Sin grows up.** The sin gets bigger and establishes a greater stronghold in your life.
7. **Something dies.** If this cycle continues to go on without ever changing, at the minimum, a part of your God-given destiny is forfeited.

You have probably already figured out that the key to overcoming temptation is to catch it in the beginning. You have to learn to see the ramifications of step seven all the way back in step one. We can't leave the temptation to take care of itself. When temptation is presented to us, its goal is to bring destruction. Sometimes things that we are tempted by seem small and insignificant, but you can't look at them while they are small—you have to consider what they will be when fully grown.

A grizzly bear cub is so cute and cuddly when it's born. But if you revisit it after it grows up, I guarantee it will be slightly less teddy-bearish than before. The key is to deal with things when they are small enough to handle so you won't be fighting for your life in the future.

Overcoming temptation is about mastering self, channeling desire in the right direction, not entertaining the slightest pulls away from purpose, and living life strategically. If you know that you are naturally inclined to lean in a certain direction, do things that prop you up in the opposite direction. Put trusted people in your life who are advocates of your destiny. Tell them when you are struggling and give them permission to question you about your progress. Write down the reasons why you are committed to not giving in to certain desires and meditate on them daily. Feed the part of you that you want to grow and starve the things that are enemies to your destiny. Study your behavior. What are you doing when you are more inclined to yield to temptation? Where are you? What are you watching or listening to? Cut those things out and replace them with things that strengthen you and affirm you in the awesome things that God has for you. You can win the temptation battle—it just takes discipline.

God's epic idea for you includes you finishing well, and *that* you will do. It won't be easy, but it will be worth it. You'll have to make some tough decisions at times, but in the end you'll be glad you did. Stay inspired and encouraged. If you make a mistake don't come down on yourself. Dust yourself off and get back up. As long as you are alive there is an opportunity to get back on the path of purpose. Learn to hear the cheers of heaven encouraging you on at all times. God believes in you and is committed to seeing you through. Forget those things that are behind, thrust full speed ahead, and finish your race strong.

Chapter 18

NEVER NOT CHANGE

Now Abraham was old, well advanced in age; and the LORD had blessed Abraham in all things. (Genesis 24:1)

The purpose journey is an amazing voyage that spans an entire lifetime. It's full of seasons and experiences that finally bring you into everything God promised you from the start. The passage above fast-forwards us into Abraham's future after spending several decades walking out his purpose with God. There is no way Abraham could've known when he started his journey to purpose that his life would be enhanced the way it was. We don't know much about Abraham's life before God engaged him at age seventy-five, but I can tell you this—his true life hadn't even begun until he stepped into his purpose. The passage reveals that Abraham lived a good long life and that God had blessed him in all things. It was like discovering his purpose gave him an extension on the life he had, and this extension would turn out to be the most meaningful and rewarding part.

Everything God said He would do in Abraham's life, and even more, had come to pass, but not without a cost to Abraham. What was the price that Abraham had to pay? What did he have to sacrifice? What did it cost him to live the type of life that most people only dream about living? The truth is, there were many sacrifices Abraham made. He had to leave the familiar. He honed his gift of good-bye. He even took several leaps of faith. But there was one consistent sacrifice that remained throughout Abraham's entire journey. It was the *one* thing he constantly had to do. Abraham had to sacrifice the comfort that most people find in *not* changing. Abraham's ultimate cost was his willingness to change in an instant, if God would so direct.

Abraham's whole journey was one of change. He had to change his environment and his surroundings. He had to make changes in his relationships. He had to change his way of thinking, and God even changed his name. Change was the one constant in Abraham's life, and this was the number one reason God could bring him into all He had for him.

The Well of Perfection

There was a certain city that Abraham spent a lot of time in. The name of that city was Beersheba. A lot of significant things in Abraham's life happened there. He seemed to be drawn to Beersheba and even bought land there. He built a place to worship God in Beersheba, and it is believed to be the place where Abraham settled down.

What's interesting about Beersheba is what its name actually means. In most cultures, names mean something. People and places aren't named arbitrarily; they have significance to the one who named them. Abraham gave Beersheba its name, and the meaning sheds light on Abraham's perspective about change.

Beersheba means "well of seven." Seven is the number of perfection or completion. A well represents a continuous flow. What Abraham was saying by naming his favorite place the well of completion was that he was calling *change* his new home. He knew the only way he could become who God said he was, would be through constant change and continuous growth. Abraham embraced a lifestyle of perpetual transformation, and was being perfected by every change he experienced. Every time a change cycle was completed, he was perfected further toward the epic idea God had revealed to him. The only thing Abraham wasn't willing to change was his commitment to change itself.

One of the reasons people find it difficult to believe what God promises is because they fail to expect change. God often comes to us at points in our lives and promises a future that is drastically different from our present. When this happens, if you aren't careful you could base the likelihood of that future on your present circumstances. Be careful to never allow what *is* to determine what *will be*. This way of thinking will keep you in yesterday when God is seeking to pull you into tomorrow. You have to allow what God speaks to you to become your new vision of what will be. Then all you have to do is be like Abraham and embrace a lifestyle of change and growth, until what will be becomes what is.

Change and Reconciliation

It's believed by many scholars that Abraham's family may have become a little dysfunctional because of a certain misunderstanding. There was a time during Abraham's life when God tested him to see where his deepest loyalty was. This test involved Abraham's willingness to sacrifice his son; the only problem was, no one knew it was a test. From the outside looking in, you see what looks like a madman tying up his young son and raising a knife to kill him. We often think about how hard it must have been for Abraham to do it but fail to consider the scarring effect it had on his son, Isaac. For it to look like you're getting ready to die brutally by the hands of the one who is supposed to provide for and protect you, must have been an extremely confusing and traumatic experience. Of course we know how the story plays out; God doesn't allow it to happen and Abraham passes the test. What we don't think about is whether or not he passes another test; a test of loyalty his scarred son and distraught wife would grade him on.

By one misunderstanding, a family is shattered. You might be thinking, "Why didn't Abraham just explain it to them? Perhaps if they had all the facts they would understand." Good question, however, there's nothing in Scripture that suggests Abraham did not try to explain. It's quite possible that he did, but to no effect. Sometimes even when you try to explain yourself, people for whatever reason still won't understand. Abraham's obedience to God had placed him in a difficult spot; one I'm sure he wondered if he would ever be able to recover from.

In the meantime, Abraham prospered in unprecedented ways. He became very rich, gaining so much influence in the region that kings bowed to him. He evolved in God's plan for his life, and with the exception of things at home, he was right on schedule with everything God had promised.

After some time, Sarah, Abraham's estranged wife, died, and he traveled to the city she lived in to bury her. Isaac, meanwhile, took it extremely hard. For him, not only did he *lose* his dad because of the misunderstanding, but he lost his mom whom he clung to tightly because of what he experienced at the hands of his father. Isaac was depressed beyond comfort and hardly came out of his mother's tent, where he made his home.

Up to this point the Scriptures describe no true interaction between Abraham and his son Isaac. Perhaps Abraham had given up on the prospect of reconciliation and just allowed things to be what they were. But when Sarah died and he witnessed the effect it was having on his son, I believe something snapped inside of him. He realized he had to do everything he could to reconcile, especially since he knew his own time of death was swiftly approaching. Abraham does so by finding a wife for his son Isaac and bestowing unto him all that he had acquired in his lifetime. There is no indication about whether or not Abraham's efforts brought them to the point of reconciliation. We do know, however, that Isaac was finally comforted after his mother's death by the wife that came into his life by the hands of his father.

I tell this story to make one point clear. If you are truly changing, evolving, and maturing, you'll undoubtedly discover things in your past you'll want to reconcile. As you embrace a lifestyle of change and becoming, you'll consider decisions you've made or actions you took that are no longer consistent with the *you* that you've become. You may have said something to someone you now regret, or ended a relationship in a not-so-pleasant way. You are not *that* person anymore and shouldn't feel condemned, but you should do everything in your power to make things right.

Abraham could've easily become proud and blamed the strained relationship on Isaac's immaturity. Although this would have been true, it's not the position he decides to take. He chooses instead to humble himself. When you are truly changing into who God is making you, along with your great strength also comes great humility. True humility is taking the strength you've been given and using it to strengthen those who are weak—even weak as a result of their own ignorance.

It's not uncommon to be misunderstood when you decide to walk out your purpose with God. No matter how hard you try, you won't be able to fix every situation, but you should still do your best to try. It doesn't take much to pick up the phone or drop a card in the mail. You'd be surprised how far it could go toward reconciliation. If someone is coming to mind right now, consider giving them a call just to show that you care. Perhaps it's a parent, friend, or former business associate. You've got nothing to lose, and who knows, you may get to experience the joy of reconciliation and the blessing that follows. A huge part of the change process is the commitment to bringing reconciliation to areas that may have been damaged in your past.

Learning to Reinvent Yourself

The life that is lived to the fullest is the life that is continuously being reinvented. There is a saying that I use often when speaking to people about purpose. I tell them, "You will never be a has-been if you learn how to reinvent yourself within the evolution of your purpose." We discussed in an earlier chapter the fact that your purpose is on the move. That means that in order to keep up with it, you've got to be on the move also. Purpose doesn't stop because we decide we're more comfortable with the last season than we are about pursuing what purpose has in store for us in the next one. Our purpose will move without our permission, and if we don't move with it, we can easily become irrelevant.

Our purpose in life is the thing that makes us relevant to the world we live in. Our purpose will always be up to date, no matter what age we may be. We just have to make sure that we are up to date with our purpose.

Here in Hollywood it's not uncommon to see men and women in their seventies trying to live the way they lived in their twenties. I am a firm believer in being young at heart and keeping yourself together no matter what your age, but when you get older and you don't embrace who've you become, the world is deprived of the great treasure you've evolved to be.

There is glory in every season and at every age. There's the glory of the newborn and the glory of the teenager. There is something special about our lives at twenty-five and a mature beauty at forty. Even fifty has significance and to be eighty years old is a blessing. For every time and season there is a purpose and meaning, and we must be diligent to inquire about our significance, in the moment we are presently living in. Reinventing yourself comes down to three questions: (1) Who am I now? (2) What world am I living in? and (3) What have I become, learned, or acquired at this point that will be a blessing to it? You will be amazed at how asking these three simple questions will put you in position to reinvent yourself in purpose and make you not only relevant to the world around you, but a great asset in it. God longs to answer these questions at every juncture of your life. Your purpose guide, the Holy Spirit, is waiting to answer every purpose-related question you could ever imagine. You have been set up for life.

Remember your best and brightest days are always in front of you. When God decided to wake you up this morning it's because He's not finished with you. His awesome plans for your life are not yet complete. What keeps you forever young is your ability to keep up with the epic idea that motivated your birth. Whenever you find your purpose, you'll find freshness, vitality, and renewal. Discovering purpose in every season is like being born all over again. It never gets old or stale, and every round, no matter what age, goes higher and higher.

The journey of purpose is one of growth, evolution, and change. Always resist rigidity, keep an open mind, and never be unwilling to evolve. One of the greatest lessons that the journey of purpose has taught me is to never *not* change.

Regardless of where you've come from or where you presently stand, your life is getting ready to become greater than it's ever been. Remember, the one area you can't fail at in life is your purpose. Before God put you in your mother's womb, He knew you and ordained you. That means that the real you will always work. You're an original and there is nobody like you—not even close. It's time for you to go for it. It's time to run your race. All of heaven is backing you up and cheering you on. Your purpose is your life. It's the reason you were born, and it's altogether epic!

ACKNOWLEDGMENTS

I'd like to give thanks and honor to the countless people who played a vital part in bringing *Purpose Awakening* to fruition. I'd first like to acknowledge the kindest woman ever, Lori Roberts, and my three amazing children who selflessly allowed me to spend a great deal of time away to get this done. I couldn't have done it without you. Thank you also to Tommye Williams, my mom and number one fan, who saw in me what I once couldn't. Thank you for encouraging me in everything I do. Thank you, Dad, for giving me the wisdom and the wherewithal to finish what I started. I love you. I want to give a special thanks to the executive staff of One Church International and the Artist Resource Center for picking up the slack when I went away to write. Thank you for keeping our operations running smoothly while I was gone. To Crystal Flores, one of my *purpose mates*, thank you for your hard work and for helping me to discover my writing voice. *Purpose Awakening* would have never happened had you not shown up in my office that day. To Jana Burson and the Hachette/FaithWords team, thank you for your professionalism, kindness, and for seeing the possibilities and potential of *Purpose Awakening*. To my brother, DeVon Franklin, thank you for your consistent inspiration and support to me while writing *Purpose Awakening*. And last but not least, thank you to the Everlasting God who awakened me to my purpose. Thank you for inspiring and enabling this book. I pray that *Purpose Awakening* brings the revelation of your great love to countless lives. I love You!